REMAKING COMMUNITY?

For Jess

Remaking Community?
New Labour and the Governance of Poor Neighbourhoods

ANDREW WALLACE
London School of Hygiene and Tropical Medicine, UK

R **Routledge**
Taylor & Francis Group

LONDON AND NEW YORK

First published 2010 by Ashgate Publishing

2 Park Square, Milton Park, Abingdon, Oxon OX14 4RN
711 Third Avenue, New York, NY 10017, USA

Routledge is an imprint of the Taylor & Francis Group, an informa business

First issued in paperback 2016

British Library Cataloguing in Publication Data
Wallace, Andrew.
  Remaking community? : New Labour and the governance of poor
neighbourhoods.
  1. Marginality, Social--Great Britain. 2. Urban poor--
Government policy--Great Britain. 3. Community
development, Urban--Great Britain. 4. Great Britain--
Social policy--1979- 5. Great Britain--Politics and
government--1997-2007. 6. Great Britain--Politics and
government--2007-
  I. Title
  361.6'1'0941-dc22

Library of Congress Cataloging-in-Publication Data
Wallace, Andrew, 1979-
  Remaking community? : New Labour and the governance of poor neighbourhoods / by Andrew
Wallace.
    p. cm.
  Includes bibliographical references and index.
  ISBN 978-0-7546-7854-0 (hbk)
  1. Community development--Great Britain. 2. Poverty--Government policy--Great Britain. 3.
Public welfare--Great Britain. 4. Great Britain--Social policy--1979- 5. Great Britain--Politics
and government--1997-2007. 6. Labour Party (Great Britain) I. Title.
  HN400.C6W35 2010
  307.3'3620869420941--dc22
                                                                              2010017358
ISBN 978-0-7546-7854-0 (hbk)
ISBN 978-1-138-25154-0 (pbk)

Contents

Preface and Acknowledgements

The genesis of this book lies in research undertaken at the University of Leeds between 2002 and 2006 and I will always be indebted to the support and direction I was offered by colleagues whilst working there. I am particularly grateful for the encouragement and advice imparted by Alan Deacon and Kirk Mann, both of whom afforded me space and autonomy to develop my ideas and get on with the job, combined with some gentle prodding when my instinct may have been endless procrastination and tinkering. Many thanks are also due to Pete Dwyer and Simon Prideaux who were supportive throughout my time at Leeds and were always willing to offer advice when approached. More recently, thanks are extended to Peter Taylor-Gooby who offered support and insight when trying to develop and transform my ideas into a publishable manuscript.

Researching and writing the book would have been a markedly different experience but for the co-operation of my interviewees, many of whom were accommodating and engaging beyond what I could have possibly hoped. I remain indebted to those who showed a willingness to talk and engage with me when, frankly, they had more important things to do.

I would also like to thank friends old and new who have helped – in their own ways – to get me to this stage, through both direct support and interest, or their ability to offer distractions and diversions. Jess, my Mum, Dad and Valerie have all offered kind words and support throughout and showed faith in me which helped me survive some inevitable wobbles and decide that, yes, I really did want to do this.

Of course, despite all of these influences the work is my own and as such any faults, flaws or faux pas are entirely of my own making.

Andrew Wallace
March 2010

List of Abbreviations

ABI	Area-based initiative
ASBO	Antisocial Behaviour Order
BBC	British Broadcasting Corporation
CCTV	Close Circuit Television
CDP	Community Development Project
CHAP	Community Health Action Partnership
CRESR	Centre for Regional, Economic and Social Research
DSS	Department of Social Security
DTTO	Drug Treatment and Testing Order
DWP	Department for Work and Pensions
HMRF	Housing Market Renewal Fund
JRF	Joseph Rowntree Foundation
LSP	Local Strategic Partnership
MIRAS	Mortgage Interest Tax Relief at Source
NDC	New Deal for Communities
NIMBY	Not-in-my-backyard
NRU	Neighbourhood Renewal Unit
ODPM	Office of the Deputy Prime Minister
PA	Participatory Appraisal
PALS	People and Life Support in Sneinton
PCT	Primary Care Trust
RSL	Registered Social Landlord
SEU	Social Exclusion Unit
SRB	Single Regeneration Budget
TSO	The Stationery Office

Chapter 1
Introduction

Preamble

My first objective in writing this book was to try to locate and disentangle its narrative threads to provide a sense of the book's scope and critical preoccupations. I felt it would be useful to begin by drawing back from the details of my inquiry and paint a wider picture of what the book would be 'about' through an early demarcation of its intellectual terrain. In light of this, my first chapter is designed to take the reader through the contexts and concerns which infuse, frame and provide the dynamic of the book. As such, I hope clear, consistent themes emerge from these initial discussions to provide something of a central thrust to the arguments posited throughout, touching as they do upon matters of government, citizenship, poverty and the sociology of community life.

Put simply, the book is concerned with projects of government that seek to affect social and behavioural change in and of poor citizens and their lived spaces. In this discussion, the key milieu is the poor neighbourhood and the use of regeneration initiatives as socio-political mechanisms to transform the spaces and places of the poor. The wider context is the opening up of new sites of governance – or 'publics' (Newman and Clarke 2009) through which new citizenships are being forged, opportunities for individual and community 'empowerment' are being constituted and government is being rearticulated. The book is a discussion of how citizens, ensnared in these conflicting, politicised spaces, negotiate and manage the expectations that beset them when they are considered not just 'ordinary' individuals with needs, values and relationships, but 'active' agents of social transformation through which projects of government are valorised. Lurking ominously in the background to these exciting ruminations on the absorption of citizens into new forms of governance are the conditions of poverty, exclusion and neglect that structure and shape the lives of so many of these newly 'active' individuals. The ensuing discussion of individual agency and the state therefore is firmly situated within an account of material, cultural and political disadvantage and I am concerned to explore how these conditions influence how residents respond to and experience new governance spaces.

The book conceives of New Labour's New Deal for Communities (NDC) programme as a useful example of a regeneration mechanism designed to stimulate shifts in the local–social and as sites of hybridised, partnership governance helping to reframe local citizenship. Given the targeting of the programme at some of the most deprived electoral wards in England, it provides an opportunity to examine how the material exclusion of resident citizens influences their capacity to participate in and legitimise shifts in the political, social and cultural reality of their neighbourhoods. Therefore, the NDC programme is taken here to be a case study in both how citizens are recruited as participants in new methods of governing the social and transforming the culture of poor neighbourhoods. The locus of my discussion centres on place and spatiality, but its concerns transcend the fixity of neighbourhood to address the models of agency, community and exclusion which, I argue, structure how NDC as a transformative project conceives, maps and constitutes local spaces and their inhabitants. I argue they underpin an instrumental regenerative dynamic designed to draw in citizens to particular social and political formations. However, I take issue with these and problematise them as limited constructions which fail to take full account of the various nuances and difficulties which frame and constrain the realisation of this dynamic. Community is of particular interest, what with the attendant problems, complexities, challenges and opportunities which flow from considerations of it as both an abstract concept infusing policymaking, and as a material, socio-spatial context for everyday living. A succinct introductory explanation of the book's subject matter therefore, should also assert its interest in community and how it is conceptualised, applied, constructed, misunderstood, exploited, experienced, contested, mobilised and activated. The book tries to unpick and analyse these impinging forces or structures *on* 'community' by way of understanding – as the title suggests – how disadvantaged neighbourhoods and those who reside in them, shape and are shaped by this most problematic of concepts. This discussion bleeds into that of individual agency and how the capabilities of resident citizens are shaped by and help shape the communities that they inhabit and the poverty that they experience. Under New Labour, community was a key site at which both new forms of governance were negotiated and the moralisation and activation of poor citizens was operationalised. Community raises therefore, not only fascinating questions in its own right, but is an important concept and field of study for any evaluation of New Labour social policy.

Suffice to say at this stage therefore, that the book is not about evaluating the technical impact of NDC programmes on the key outcomes mandated by central government. The national evaluation of NDC (see DCLG 2008; CRESR 2009a; 2009b; 2009c; Lawless et al. 2009) provides some important context and colour to my discussion of one particular NDC, but it is not my intention here to assess the impact of NDC on key performance indicators. My goal is to explore how NDC enacted socio-political shifts in poor neighbourhoods and how residents in these 'communities' experienced these shifts.

Before setting out how this discussion will unfold, I would like to begin by taking a few steps back and engaging with some of the aforementioned key themes which underpin the book. The first of these relates to the political and intellectual milieu in which my discussion of projects of New Labour government takes place.

The Rise and Fall of New Labour

The intellectual gaze of this book is fixed and shaped by the social and political agenda of the New Labour 'project' which we can roughly sketch as having played out between 1994 and 2010. The origins of writing and researching the book lie in the mid-2000s and can be located within what we might consider a British critical social policy tradition that at that time had New Labour's social welfare agenda firmly in its sights. Then, New Labour was still the dominant political force in the UK and the party leadership's craven accommodation of neo-liberal economics was continuing to generate ideological and ethical disquiet from the Left, but was continuing unabated, matched with substantial social investment and interventionist social policies as yet untroubled by recession or the global credit squeeze. An important premise of my analysis is that the New Labour 'project' contained an identifiable social welfare agenda predicated on a combination of social investment and a transformation of British society. This combination comprised an identifiable though unstable socio-ethical project that prioritised economic competitiveness, civic renewal and the rebalancing of individual duties and rights, operationalised through by-now familiar New Labour policy themes: welfare to work, neighbourhood regeneration, social cohesion, community empowerment, active citizenship and civic 'respect'. For me, these themes could be mapped, understood and critically assessed as a social policy project. Therefore, in a sense the book is a fairly traditional example of social policy analysis which seeks to trace a reasonably coherent policy agenda from the ideas and analyses espoused by key New Labour politicians and thinkers through to the interventions and programmes funded by the New Labour government. Nowhere was this more apparent than in neighbourhood regeneration, which appeared to enshrine many of the dominant New Labour preoccupations – social inclusion, empowered citizens, ordered communities – in an array of policy interventions designed to tackle everything from poor housing to 'families from hell', all with the apparent purpose of 'bridging the gap' between poor communities and 'mainstream' society (SEU 1998). This analytical approach is not unproblematic and there are some who would no doubt take issue with conceptualising any policy agenda or political project in this seemingly neat way. There are further difficulties in assuming coherence between politics and the policy process, that is, how much of what happens on the ground can we really attribute to the chatter of politicians and the necessary fictions of policy documents? This is another challenge for my analysis but I contend that the intellectual origins of the New Deal for Communities (NDC) regeneration programme – the main policy intervention under scrutiny here – can be traced back in part to the (admittedly fragile and unstable) social agenda alluded to here. Indeed, NDC managed to endure throughout New Labour's period in office despite sometimes rather troubled stewardship by different central government departments and the shifting policy priorities which it had to navigate (Lawless et al. 2009).

Whilst the scope of the book is informed by an account of New Labour's impact on social welfare, it also has to grapple with New Labour's diminished political significance and policy relevance. Indeed, revisiting and analysing New Labour in 2010 feels like it has some inherent risks – not least because the 'project' has been subject to exhaustive academic and media debate, and in UK political terms, feels like an anachronism. Moreover, from the standpoint of social policy scholarship, the banking and recessionary crisis of 2008–09 altered the landscape and terms of debate dramatically. Both of these points invite us to consider both how much more there is to say about New Labour, and how much of it has any resonance with current as well as future social policy debates. This leaves the book in a peculiar position of advocating the significance of the New Labour era in social policy just as the governing project from which it derives draws its final breaths.

Of course, I hope to surmount this challenge by arguing that this is not only an opportune moment, as it is replaced by a Conservative/LibDem coalition government, to examine the contribution and effect of New Labour. I also want to assert that many of the arguments of the book transcend the existence of New Labour and I would suggest have significance beyond recent policy interventions. Whilst New Labour provides the framework, context and receives much of the critical scrutiny, it is important to stress that the book is not only about evaluating New Labour, but about offering an account of citizen – state relations that will have resonance beyond the immediate policy conditions. These accounts will continue to have relevance if, as seems likely, the Coalition Government under David Cameron continues to construct poor neighbourhoods in similar terms as problematic policy subjects whilst maintaining it's theme of empowering 'big' citizens and 're-imagining' the role of the state (Cameron 2009). Indeed, the overlapping approaches of Conservative and Labour policy can be situated not just within their own intellectual logic but within transcendent shifts in governance and a legacy of policy interventionism which has continually sought to problematise spatial concentrations of poverty; and not always in the most sympathetic terms.

The Shadow of the Slum

Another key narrative of this book is around some of the continuities in urban policy over the last century and specifically observing how 'poor' places have been consistently reproduced, discursively, as a source of unease and a 'threat' to civilised society and therefore as objects of policy intervention. For example, in the 1930s, George Orwell commented on the increasing presence of the unsettling 'slums' in policy discourse:

> ... even people with comfortable incomes are vaguely troubled by the thought of "the slums". Hence the clatter about "re-housing" and "slum clearance" which we have had at intervals ever since the war. Bishops, politicians, philanthropists and whatnot enjoy talking piously about "slum clearance", because they can

then divert attention from more serious evils and pretend that if you abolish the slums you abolish poverty (2001: 59).

Over the last eighty years or so, analyses of this concern have shifted, as have ideas about how to solve this seemingly intractable social problem. This is evinced by an examination of policy responses over this period that have sought to either manage, renew, regenerate, develop or simply demolish places of concentrated poverty, identified by commentators variously as slums, ghettoes, 'dump' or 'sink' estates or excluded neighbourhoods. However, as Hoban and Beresford have pointed out, the existence of such areas at the beginning of the new century could be 'living testimony to the failed regeneration policies of the past' (2001: 312) and illustrates how policy failure is the point around which these responses coalesce. Indeed, Orwell had prefaced this point when he noted presciently in 1937 that 'all this talk has led to surprisingly small results' (2001: 60). Therefore, another concern which plays out throughout the book is not just why this sense of the threatening slum exists, but why so little appears to have been achieved from successive policy interventions and why 'dangerous' places continue to be represented as such in policy discourse. An important part of my analysis of New Labour therefore, involves questioning the authenticity of their urban renewal efforts and locating those efforts within a broader legacy of interventions in the local spaces of the poor. My implicit position in these discussions is a sense of allegiance with such places and I am critical of the pejorative representations and failures that have been imposed upon them. My analysis therefore, does not engage too much with a positivist concern with finding the 'correct' form of intervention or solution to the 'problems' of the slum, but with a more fluid set of concerns which critique how it is that 'slums' have been constructed as a policy problem and the techniques and strategies that have been sought to map, manage and 'empower' them. For the purposes of this book, the specific focus (of the many we could choose from) is clearly New Labour's strategies and in particular, their deploying of 'community' as a tool of analysis and social change of and for the poor or 'sink' neighbourhood.

Underwriting all of the policy approaches noted above and the different analytical or political trends they reflect is a common belief at the 'high' policy level of the need to prescribe area based policy measures to 'treat' poor areas and address the conditions of those who reside in them. Therefore, despite changing social and political contexts, there have been successive programmes that have emerged, all aimed at tackling some aspect of localities designated as being in need. This process began with the fundamentalist slum clearance programmes in the 1930s, which demonstrated a belief in razing the physical habitat of the urban poor, and recently continued with New Labour's more developmental Neighbourhood Renewal agenda, which combined some physical re-development with improvements in local service delivery and a range of didactic interventions for residents of such areas, designed to encourage 'participation', 'partnership' and 'empowerment'.

Whilst it can be difficult to pin down the origins of the anxiety surrounding concentrated poverty and its consistent status as a policy concern, the belief in the need to devise area-based programmes to address it remains an important and totemic aspect of government policy. As far as New Labour is concerned, it continued this tradition and aimed to analyse and 'tackle' the problems experienced by residents of poor areas and 'Bring Britain Together' (SEU 1998):

> Over the past twenty years, hundreds of poor neighbourhoods have seen their basic quality of life become increasingly detached from the rest of society ... Many neighbourhoods have been stuck in a spiral of decline. Areas with high crime and unemployment rates acquired poor reputations, so people, shops and employers left (SEU 2001a).

However, New Labour differed from its immediate predecessors in government in some key aspects. Firstly, as Ginsburg has noted, New Labour emphasised the 'social' elements of urban regeneration and its place in wider anti-poverty agendas. The reclaiming of regeneration as a social welfare arena contrasted with previous Conservative administrations that focused on economic investment as the solution to areas perceived to be in decline (1999: 58). According to Cochrane, this reflected a New Right conviction that social welfare could not be decoupled from economic development and a questioning of the efficacy of public sector professionals (2000: 190). Moreover, New Labour constructed 'detached' poor areas not as 'deprived' as in previous eras, but as 'socially excluded.'[1] This appeared to convey residents of poor areas as both materially and spatially distinct from the 'mainstream'. New Labour's urban policy focus on 'renewing' specified 'neighbourhoods' and 'communities' was designed to bridge the 'gap' deemed to permeate both the physical and moral landscape of post-industrial Britain. Only identifying and 'renewing' these areas (thereby closing the gap) would produce the orderly, inclusive and productive society New Labour desired. From this viewpoint, the neighbourhood renewal agenda is one that fitted with broader welfare objectives derived from a distinctive New Labour social vision founded upon reframing the relationship between citizen and state (Clarke 2005; Heron and Dwyer 1999; Lund 1999).

Given the sustained policy interest in spatial manifestations of poverty over recent years, it is perhaps surprising that there have been apparently few attempts in the academic literature to fully explain this trend. However, there appear to be a number of critical frameworks to analyse this interest nonetheless. For example, one framework would be to adopt the radical argument that the policy agenda is controlled by agents of elitist or bourgeois control whereby the consent of the 'dangerous classes' for the iniquities of capitalism is maintained through localised

---

1   Although it defined poor areas via indices of multiple deprivation illustrating that the term still had validity.

poverty programmes. Cochrane has explained what is known as 'gilding the ghetto' (Community Development Project 1977):

> From this perspective the role of urban policy was to make cities safe (and productive) for "global capitalism", to manage the conflicts within them and particularly to manage the poor or the socially excluded, so that they did not disrupt the processes of social and economic restructuring (2000: 200).

Robert Furbey has attempted to theorise successive government's preoccupation with poor places. That is, what lies behind the anxiety provoked by areas of poverty or perceived squalor and the subsequent need to 'regenerate' (or demolish)? In response, he argues firstly that it derives from a fear on the part of the nineteenth century establishment, but still resonating today, of the physical and moral effects of living in the 'stunting environmental slums' (1999: 426).[2] Stedman Jones illustrates some of these fears by citing several observers of the time who highlighted the apparent effects of 'decaying slum life' (1971: 287). For example, in 1886 Lord Brabazon wrote: 'Let the reader walk through the wretched streets ... should he be of average height, he will find himself a head taller than those around him; he will see on all sides pale faces, stunted figures, debilitated forms ...' (cited in Stedman Jones 1971: 308). Secondly, Furbey suggests that respectable fears about the 'stunting' effects reflected concerns about 'the evolution of the social organism' (1999: 426). Here Furbey locates anxiety about 'the slums' (and resultant urban policymaking) in two schools of nineteenth century thought: Social Darwinism and Enlightenment Organicism. He argues that those who subscribed to such thinking constructed concentrations of poverty as an 'ailment' of the social body to be 'treated'. If 'unmedicated', there would be consequences for the progression of society as a whole, destined perhaps, to remain as 'uncivilised' as its poorest extremities. Stedman Jones suggests that a 'theory of degeneration' in the 1880s succeeded in shifting middle class analysis of poverty from moral inadequacy to 'the deleterious influences of the urban environment' (1971: 313). It became clear, he suggests, that poverty and degeneracy had to become concerns of the state as the sense of threat from the presence and possible spread of an impoverished mass began to grow (1971: 313). The most recent example of the degeneracy discourse is perhaps the Conservative Party's rhetoric around the 'broken' society – a diagnosis that explicitly attempts to delineate a problem periphery with threatening implications for the 'healthy' mainstream (Centre for Social Justice 2006).

Furbey continues by arguing that the theoretical fusion that created this physiological metaphor re-emerged in early Fabian fears of moral deterioration and then in later social democratic interventions into the 'welfare' of the poor (1999: 426). Certainly, poor areas are often described and rhetorically mapped

---

2   A concern that resonates in today's 'neighbourhood effects' debate (For example, Atkinson and Kintrea 2001).

by politicians and planners through a range of negative motifs such as 'disorder', 'spiral of decline', 'cycles of deprivation', 'overcrowding' and 'exclusion'. This may be to accentuate their 'otherness' and diagnose the problems apparently peculiar to these spaces thereby differentiating them from 'healthy' (social) body parts. An excerpt from Jim Callaghan, then Home Secretary, explaining the Government's new Urban Aid programme in 1968 is typical of the way poor spaces are constructed: 'It is intended to arrest ... and reverse the downward spiral which afflicts so many of these areas. There is a deadly quagmire of need and apathy' (Community Development Project 1977: 10). Here we see the construction of poor spaces as defective and stunting terrain. There is a subtext of moral deterioration and a belief in the need for the state to intervene and 'treat' an ingrained cultural pathology. Therefore, urban renewal programmes can be seen as attempts to challenge a 'culture' of poverty and the pathology of poor residents and intercept the intergenerational transmission of poverty (Lupton 2003: 9). In this case, programmes reflect a judgement about the inherently feckless character of the poor or the corrosion of their character by poverty (see for example, Wilson 1987). Either way, residents have no role other than as passive policy subjects who are a problem to be solved by programmes devised by 'experts'.

Conversely, a more sympathetic analysis would suggest such programmes actually represent a genuine attempt to repair some of the social and economic trauma inflicted by industrial upheaval and improve the conditions of those who live in affected areas. Furthermore, one could say they demonstrate the success of residents or community workers in placing the conditions of their areas onto the central Government policymaking radar. Indeed, perhaps it is short-sighted to always view urban regeneration programmes as a domain purely of the welfare professions where social problems are selected for treatment from on high. The potential influence of claims made on government resources by the poor themselves or those who work with them cannot be discounted in an analysis of policy responses. This was seen most clearly in the late 1960s, when community work became a mechanism by which central regeneration policy was questioned and subverted at the local level (Cochrane 2000: 190). The Community Development Project, set up by the Home Office under the auspices of Jim Callaghan in 1969 embodied this tension. Those workers who were employed by the state to investigate and 'help' designated poor areas found themselves 'going native' to some extent and undermining some of the assumptions of the welfare professionals and clashing with local authorities and politicians, ostensibly their employers (Community Development Project 1977: 4).

In contemporary terms, we can perhaps locate New Labour's preoccupation with socially excluded neighbourhoods within bits of all these explanatory frameworks. There are certainly those who would characterise regeneration programmes such as the NDC as vehicles for neo-liberal restructuring and 'empowering' residents in social projects which not only fail to challenge the power relations which determine their poverty, but function to compound or obscure that poverty (Amin 2005). Furthermore, the metaphor of the malfunctioning social body is perhaps identifiable in the adoption of the concept of social exclusion and the fear in neighbourhoods and people being 'cut off' from mainstream society, a situation considered morally unacceptable as well as socially problematic and economically wasteful (SEU 2001b). As Tony Blair noted: 'Over the past two decades the gap between the 'worst' estates and the rest of the country has grown. It has left us with a situation that no civilised country should tolerate ... [and] we all have to pay for the costs' (SEU 1998: 1, brackets added). This may or may not reflect New Labour's alleged commitment to a quasi-functionalist philosophy (see, for example, Levitas 1998; Prideaux 2001), one that derived from the same body of Enlightenment thought Furbey discusses. Nonetheless, New Labour had obvious concerns about the negative effects of living in one of the 'worst' estates and made a commitment that no citizens should be seriously disadvantaged by where they live (SEU 2001b). New Labour mapped out with familiar language the seemingly inevitable processes that cause neighbourhoods to decline:

> As areas become unpopular, those who can move out do so and families with little choice move in. As a result, the area becomes poorer ... For those who live in these areas, prolonged spells out of work can lead to disaffection and exclusion, and a lack of commitment to the area. This may lead to more crime and vandalism, which leads to further decline (DSS 1999, cited in Deacon 2003).

Therefore, the New Labour government conceived of socially excluded areas as a concern both because they symbolise a divided, perhaps malfunctioning society and because such conditions contribute to reducing the quality of life of residents. Urban regeneration programmes were in part therefore, ethical projects designed to offer genuine assistance to residents. It could also be argued that in devising urban programmes, New Labour responded to a growing sense that tackling poverty must involve recognising and respecting the voices and experiences of the poor (Lister 2002), hence the emphasis on 'involving' and 'empowering' communities. The implication being that the poor succeeded in arguing for their collective participation in anti-poverty measures and New Labour responded with an array of opportunities for their engagement.

Whatever the explanation, a key premise of this book is that New Labour deployed a particular model of community to underpin their attempts to address the exclusion of deprived neighbourhoods. This model was a construct of social and economic relations that was designed to transform the individual and collective behaviour of excluded residents. New Labour attempted to ameliorate the problems of decaying places and their contingent defective cultures through transformations in the local-social and the application of community. A key task of the book will be to explain this process and locate it within New Labour's broader welfare agenda as well as the legacy of fears about the slum identified here.

Questioning Community

In addition to situating the contours of New Labour's policy approach to poor neighbourhoods, another important theme of this book is investigating how community is lived and experienced; in particular, how it is lived and experienced in the kind of 'threatening' places that loom so large in the policy discourses noted above. The method I employ in conducting this investigation means that a large part of the book bears some of the hallmarks of a controversial method of social research: the community study. However, at no point in designing or conducting the field research (the data from which forms a substantial part of this book) did I have any pretensions to engage in anything as ambitious, or perhaps as unattainable as 'studying' a community as a totality. It is more accurate to say that the book is engaged with the living and doing of 'community' and to some degree is concerned with going 'in search' of community (Brent 2009). Whilst taking account of the difficulties inherent in separating social and spatial forms; the book attempts to conceive of 'community' as a narrative, discourse, cultural resource or political formation which can be mobilised, resisted or celebrated by residents who inhabit a bounded geographical space. To this end, if I am referring in the book to a geographical entity, then I use the term 'neighbourhood' to try and loosen the relationship between geographical and social space. Of course, this is a relationship which cannot be obscured – and we shall see later in the book how it can be central to making individual or group claims to community – so I do not seek here to claim that geographical space is socially neutral. Rather, I express doubt about the way in which New Labour policy mobilised a model of social relations that overplayed the significance of the spatial and I seek some intellectual leg room in which to examine 'community' as a politicised social space in which various processes and relations transcend and unsettle this spatial determinism.

As this stance would suggest, a key refrain throughout the book is my dissatisfaction with community as it is constructed by much academic and policy discourse and it is clear that my research questions and field research decisions grew explicitly out of that dissatisfaction. My suspicions around what I consider a banal model of community deployed by New Labour to map, manage and transform the local-social inspired me to want to visit an actually-existing neighbourhood and engage in research which expressed some of the rhythms and complexities of social existence and emphasised the emotions, conflicts and imperfections that infuse that existence. To some extent, I set out to challenge and demystify a spatially-determined model of community that appeared to provide little space for the influence of other constitutive social processes on how people interact and behave either individually or collectively. My starting point followed the work of Hoggett (1997) and Brent (1997) amongst others which emphasised the contested, complex nature of local, collective life and my particular focus was on the role played by conflict and difference and the ruptures of place and space that frame how individuals experience that life. Therefore,

I was interested in examining particular kinds of relationships and experiences and how they were negotiated by residents – in other words, examining, in part, how they 'did' their community. I thought an ideal setting for this study would be a neighbourhood that Government itself had identified as worthy and in need of policy intervention.

A key setting for the book therefore is the neighbourhood in Greater Manchester I spent many months visiting, attending meetings and arranging to interview residents and local activists. This was a 'socially excluded' area designated in 2001 to receive New Deal for Communities regeneration funding to address some of its disadvantages and alleged problems. The focus of the field research was on how residents experienced living in this particular neighbourhood, with a particular interest in three sets of relationships:

- the relationship between residents and their neighbourhood – the interplay of physical, social and political factors that shape the environment in which they lived;
- the relationship between residents – how did individuals and groups perceive each other, relate to each other and behave towards each other?
- the relationship between residents and the NDC programme – how did its ideas and practices impinge upon local people and how did they respond?

The purpose of investigating these relationships was to engage with and understand how community is understood and practised by residents in an area constructed by Government policy as needing physical, social and cultural intervention and renaissance. It was to examine the extent to which the experiences and meanings of community as expressed by residents bore any resemblance to the model of community practised and promoted by the NDC programme. Community is therefore the central terrain of the book as I compare how it was mobilised in and through policy as a mechanism of regeneration with how it was experienced and mobilised by residents in the case study neighbourhood. The material setting of this study was an NDC neighbourhood in which the houses, roads, shops, cars, river, school and park were all key sites in the living and negotiation of community, but the analytical focus of the book is on divergent readings of community as a socio-cultural narrative, practice or resource: one as a basis for and means of state-sponsored urban regeneration and the other as a means of making sense of and negotiating everyday life. In this sense, my analysis is in the tradition of 'bottom-up' social enquiry in which the voices and experiences of recipients of policy are fore-grounded as part of an examination of policy development and impact, although I was all too aware (and some of the data used here will confirm) of my status as 'outsider' and researcher bringing my own assumptions, concerns and problematics to bear on local meanings and experiences of community.

Resident Citizens and the State

One of the key criticisms of community studies as a method is their reductionism. Several scholars have noted the tendency of researchers to treat their subject communities as stand-alone entities without sufficient attention to the structures of power that can suffuse neighbourhoods and shape how residents experience and relate to each other (see Day 2006). This can be contrasted with more embedded analyses of community in which places and residents are situated within broader economic and social relations which circumscribe their everyday life and from a politicised perspective, often constrain the ability of the poor to exercise autonomy and control over their lives (for example, Amin 2005). This is not about rights to material resources – important though they are – but about recognising that a lack of citizen autonomy is an important constituent of poverty and that it can be structural: created and maintained by state-sponsored attempts to control, police or 'nudge' individuals into particular social formations. This type of analysis resonates with some Marxist and poststructuralist readings of the state in which it is viewed as a key actor or site in the continued definition and oppression of subaltern people and spaces. These concerns invite us to consider the activities of the state and, in this case, examine how it seeks to build and transform communities within poor neighbourhoods. It situates government attempts to construct and activate new forms of individual and collective being through the prescription of community within clear critical parameters. Firstly, we must consider the impact of NDC on local people implicitly defined as suffering from past government neglect and economic disadvantage. Furthermore, we need to question the social justice contribution of regeneration practice and the extent to which it enhances the ability of residents to exercise autonomy and control over their individual and collective lives. Whilst a programme like NDC can be considered a compensatory response to state and market failure and is an explicit recognition of the hardships faced by residents, it is important to consider whether it empowers residents in any meaningful way. This places even greater scrutiny on the supposedly empowering, transformative effects of the NDC programme. Broadening our scope slightly, it also places in scrutiny the civic renewal agenda pursued by New Labour and the emphasis on civility, respect and behaviour that constitute key strategies in producing ordered spaces.

Secondly, if we adopt a poststructuralist position we need to question the meaning of government interventions such as NDC in poor spaces and whether they can be assessed in justice terms at all if they are indelible techniques of advanced liberal government (Rose 1999). This could be a useful analytical framework in aiding our understanding of why programmes like NDC function in the way they do and why they have a chequered history when it comes to expanding and securing the freedom of poor spaces (Taylor 2003). Certainly, the Foucauldian critique would be that the goal is not and has never been to enhance citizen freedom per se, but to inscribe and frame that 'freedom' in particular ways in order to enable a rearticulating of the role of the state.

An important layer of my investigation in this book therefore, considers how the NDC programme affects opportunities for the achievement of greater autonomy and social justice for residents. This involves examining what political implications the model of community mobilised to intervene in the allegedly defective or disadvantaged culture of poor neighbourhoods had for residents. This is to argue that the arrival of NDC engenders the interplay of divergent readings of community that constitutes a relationship between residents and the NDC as residents are drawn into the gaze of the NDC programme, which is explicit about involving and empowering residents as transformative agents in the process of regeneration (MacLeavy 2009). Under what is constructed in policy documents as a fairly benign and benevolent NDC programme, residents are constructed as active participants who can reflect upon their disadvantage and craft strategies and solutions to their social exclusion. However, it there is some unease that NDC in fact introduced a further structural impediment to the improvement of resident's lives – not so much through the creation of the regenerated neighbourhood as a neo-liberal 'space' as suggested by Brenner and Theodore (2002), but as an additional relation of power to be negotiated in the practice of 'doing' community and realising organic 'journeys of empowerment' (Warren-Adamson cited in Dinham 2005: 303). This operated in two ways. Firstly, in overtly seeking to affect change in the norms and expectations of residents, the danger was that NDC favoured particular social formations and expressions of social action that ran counter to the needs and/or desires of residents. Secondly, by circumscribing specific modes of community expression, NDC ran the risk of compounding the disadvantages experienced by residents. By embedding NDC in a restrictive model of community designed as a means of tackling poverty and exclusion, New Labour appeared to threaten potential opportunities for greater autonomy, ownership and social justice on the part of residents, A major theme of the book therefore is not just comparing how community is practised by people with how it is mobilised by policy but also examining the political implications of that tension for residents.

The Structure of the Book

Hopefully, these opening paragraphs have provided a flavour of the concerns and preoccupations that infuse the book and give an idea of the main themes for discussion. The next chapter begins my discussion by providing an account of the development and philosophical standpoints of New Labour and traces how neighbourhood renewal was an agenda that derived from the reframing of welfare during the New Labour administrations. This discussion involves looking at three key concepts of community, responsibility and opportunity. Chapter 3 builds on this, but introduces a slightly different analytical approach in that it explores theories of governance which argue that policymaking and implementation have been dispersed to an array of sub national sites. I argue that this is a useful way of thinking about NDC, although I my response to the governance agenda is a cautious one. Nonetheless, it is considered here to have some explanatory value when thinking about how NDC both constitutes localities as communities and local residents as active, transformative agents. The rest of the chapter begins to unpack NDC in more detail, looking more closely at its design and conceptual underpinning before providing an introduction to the fieldwork experience in an NDC neighbourhood which provides the data in later chapters.

Chapter 4, having set out what I think are the key intellectual and policy contexts and drivers of the NDC programme, is the first of three chapters which takes one of the key NDC concepts of community, agency and exclusion and analyses how it was operationalised by NDC and draws on academic literature to problematise how it was deployed by New Labour. Beginning with community, each of these chapters begins with some exposition of how the concept infused the NDC approach, moves on to explore the critical literature around each, before drawing on fieldwork data to enhance and illustrate some of the problematics I have identified. Each of these chapters offers an illuminating insight into how the assumptions and models that underpinned NDC were interpreted, contested and challenged by residents in an NDC neighbourhood. Leading on from these, Chapter 7 moves the discussion on to examine two important questions. Firstly, why, if NDC and New Labour seem to have got things wrong to the extent that I describe, was this particular neighbourhood selected for NDC funding in the first place? This is a discussion which takes us into quite different analytical territory and invites us to consider the motivation of New Labour and the shifting meaning and terrain of welfare. Secondly, having examined how NDC residents appeared to be having to negotiate problematic assumptions about their culture and behaviour, what are the implications for the greater autonomy and justice in poor places ostensibly given a 'new deal' by New Labour governments. In conclusion to my discussion of NDC, I seek a judgement on New Labour and whether it empowered poor citizens in any meaningful way. Chapter 7 and my concluding chapter address these final, political questions.

Chapter 2
New Labour, New Welfare Citizens

Introduction

As noted in Chapter 1, the critical gaze of this book is to some degree framed by what is considered here to be a distinctive if unstable and inconsistent era of social welfare under successive New Labour governments. Having defined this 'era' as distinctive, one of my first goals is to do some unpacking and provide an exposition of what differentiated New Labour's welfare agenda. To this end, I provide an account of 'New Labour' as a political and philosophical project, illustrating the genesis of both its thinking and policy direction. This includes discussions of 'Third Way' concepts and strategies and how they have influenced New Labour's approach to welfare reform. Furthermore, I draw out and discuss what we might consider the key organising principles of the New Labour welfare approach and explore how New Labour sought to reframe the meaning and contours of citizenship as part of an attempt to transform the relationship between individuals and the state. The objective of this chapter is to embed specific policy programmes like NDC within a wider political and philosophical framework through which we can understand the structure and objectives of such programmes. NDC in particular is a regeneration programme which requires significant unpacking and this chapter draws attention to how it operates through reconfigurations of both community and individual agency consistent with broader concerns to enhance the functionality of the social and argues that NDC was constituted by and constituent of this broader agenda.

Two notes of caution to sound at this stage however: firstly, I am aware of the danger of presenting a glib narrative of 'New Labour' at the expense of analysis which reveals the inconsistencies and tensions inherent in the 'project'. What follows is not intended as a fully realised account of New Labour (if such a thing is possible), but an attempt to draw out where New Labour ideas and positions coalesced into a reasonably coherent governing agenda and to map the origins of that agenda. Secondly, I am wary of painting New Labour as year-zero iconoclasts wilfully scorching the UK's welfare terrain. Whilst I argue that a distinct welfare approach was in evidence, this analysis is embedded in a reading of UK social and urban policy containing various continuities and vicissitudes over time that transcend, delimit and shape the meaning and scope of politically-driven policy. One of the implicit objectives of the book is to examine the blurred relationship between political discourses and policy shifts and to assess – if possible – what contribution New Labour's welfare agenda made to policy realities during its time in office. Chapter 3 explores the embeddedness of the NDC programme, but at this stage my objective is to provide an account of the relevant political forces that shaped part of the neighbourhood renewal agenda.

The Project of 'New' Labour

It is generally considered that the political project of 'New' Labour was the culmination of a process of policy and intellectual 'modernisation' that began under Neil Kinnock in the aftermath of the watershed general election defeat of 1983 (Burden, Petrie and Cooper 2000; Fairclough 2000). The three successive Blair governments from 1997 to 2007 were the classic encapsulation of this project; popularly defined as preoccupied with media representation and a dogged occupation of the political centre-ground.[1] Ideologically, New Labour was borne of a gradual shift away from traditional 'old' Labour commitments to public ownership, Keynesian economic management and explicit wealth redistribution (Driver and Martell 2000). The architects of New Labour were keen to distance the 'modernised' party under Tony Blair from the perceived failures of post-war social democracy, whilst creating a viable, centre-Left political alternative to combat the conservative 'New Right' that had dominated British elections in the 1980s and 1990s. To some extent, the transition from 'old' to New Labour reflected an intellectual development that occurred within and without the party. A range of influences impinged on the modernising of the party and its policy direction: from reports emerging from think tanks networked into the party leadership such as Demos and the Institute for Public Policy Research, to contributions from influential commentators such as Polly Toynbee and Will Hutton. A concerted effort to reconfigure left of centre politics took place over this period, a tide of intellectual endeavour that Labour party modernisers appropriated or discarded as they felt necessary. It is worth noting however that the transformation of the Labour Party was one initiated, implemented and sustained by its leadership. Whilst one could argue that Neil Kinnock and Tony Blair enjoyed considerable support from the grassroots party membership, with the latter even able to gain consent for altering the constitution in 1995, it is important to understand 'New Labour' was a largely top-down 'modernising' exercise which produced many unresolved tensions within the party about its philosophy and direction that would play out during its years in office.

---

1   The book refers to a capitalised 'New Labour' in order to convey a sense of the political agenda under discussion. That is, the 'New Labour' brand came to symbolise a rather sanitised social-democratic narrative distinct from 'Labour' (Fairclough 2000). Indeed, the adoption of this brand became widespread in academic and media discourse as commentators deployed it, somewhat pejoratively, as part of their critical armoury – subverting party image management. 'New Labour' often became a rhetorical stick with which to beat Blairite modernisers.

Much was made of the importance placed on media presentation and political 'spin' by New Labour and concerns were expressed about the project's superficiality and lack of intellectual heft. This disquiet produced, in the worst cases, crude caricatures of a party at war with its social democratic heritage concerned with nothing more than electoral success. More considered critiques tended to focus on the pragmatic technocracy of New Labour's policy decisions and bemoaned its lack of an egalitarian imagination or 'song in their heart' (Page 2007). However, whilst it is resolutely the case that New Labour was never concerned with pursuing transformative socialist politics, it is facile to suggest that the values and goals that the project did embody could just be defined negatively (that is, not 'socialist' or 'old' Labour) or that the project amounted to nothing more than a victory of style over substance (see Scammel 2003). Of course, these were both valid concerns and partial truths, but I want to argue that New Labour actually grew to embody a distinctive set of values underpinned by various positions adopted in relation to poverty, the family, morality, community and wider social change. This value base derived from a multitude of sources ranging from strands of Christian socialism (Deacon and Mann 1997), American welfare reforms (Powell 2000; Deacon 2000), Democratic party strategies in the USA (Giddens 2000) and the social analyses provided by sociologists such as Anthony Giddens and communitarian political scientists such as Amitai Etzioni (Prideaux 2005; Deacon and Mann 1997). We cannot overlook either the influence of some key ideas from the conservative Right such as the fear of (social) welfare dependency (Lister 1998) and a belief in cycles of disadvantage (Deacon 2002a). Each of these contributed to a set of values and concerns notable for both their consistency with established political positions and their radicalism in underpinning attempts to reform and 'modernise' both state and society.

Despite sporadic tensions between key figures in the upper echelons of the party and the ebb and flow of different ideas and policy priorities, I believe it is possible to speak of a definite, synthesised New Labour project encompassing a range of beliefs and aspirations. The area of policy that garnered most discussion was probably how New Labour came to conceptualise income inequality and poverty. Seen as the litmus test of any left of centre political party, there was a glut of commentaries identifying and decrying the jettisoning of traditional 'old' Labour rhetoric about poverty and wealth redistribution, identifying how such goals were supplanted by supine 'third way' concerns with reconciling social justice with economic efficiency, 'community', equality of opportunity and social exclusion (see Levitas 1998; Lister 1998, 2000; Powell 2000, 2002; Burden, Petrie and Cooper 2000; Fairclough 2000; Page 2007). For example: 'The paradigm shift in Labour party thinking on 'welfare' can be summed up as a move away from an equality agenda to one comprising the trinity of responsibilities, inclusion and opportunity ...' (Lister 2000: 9). Similarly, Powell argued that New Labour rejected: 'both the inequality of the new right and the equality of outcome which it associates with the old left. The new goal is social inclusion' (2000: 23). It would be wrong to suggest that all of these 'third way' concerns were novel, but the relevant point is that they did indeed mark a decisive break from a recent past where the Labour party was still committed to an equality of outcomes not just opportunities and aggressive taxation of high earners. Certainly, these breaks from the past, described by Ruth Lister above, were also reflected not only in shifting policy priorities, but also in a new language used to soften the rhetoric of Labour politics. For example, when in Opposition and in the early days of government, Labour politicians were very careful not to refer to 'poverty', but to 'social exclusion' (Deacon 2003: 6).[2] Similarly, Lister noted, 'Redistribution has become the 'r' word, whose name the government dare not speak...' (2000: 10). The transition to New Labour entailed both a genuine intellectual reformation aimed at thinking differently and a pragmatic, self-conscious effort to be *seen* to be thinking differently, which required a reformation not just of ideas, but of language (Fairclough 2000). This went as far as attempts to disguise its redistributive policies from the scrutiny of 'middle England' – a conscious space opened between rhetoric and reality created to navigate competing voter tastes (Fairclough 2000: 143).

The Third Way

The Third Way was Anthony Giddens' agenda for economic and welfare reform based on his diagnosis of the challenges facing individuals and nation states in the late 20th century. It was synonymous with the renaissance of the Labour party during the 1990s and for some gave the aforementioned project of modernisation a degree of intellectual gravitas. For others, it contributed to an alarming muddying of New Labour's philosophical waters (see Cammack 2004). Nonetheless, politically the Third Way manifested in what was portrayed as a radical agenda that celebrated going 'beyond left and right' (Giddens 1994) and promised to implement 'what works' (Labour Party 1997: 4). Tony Blair allied himself closely to the Third Way and stated at the time:

> The "Third Way" is to my mind the best label for the new politics which the progressive centre-left is forging in Britain and beyond ... It is founded on the values which have guided progressive politics for more than a century – democracy, liberty, justice, mutual obligation and internationalism. But it is a third way because it moves decisively beyond an Old Left preoccupied by state control, high taxation and producer interests; and a New Right treating public investment, and often the very notions of 'society' and collective endeavour, as evils to be undone (1998: 1).[3]

---

2   The preference for talking about 'social exclusion' may also have been a preference for it as an analytical concept. Considerable debate has occurred around the efficacy of this shift (see, for example, Room 1995; Jordan 1996; Levitas 1998), but a major part of its appeal appears, nonetheless, to have been that was less evocative in voters imaginations.

3   At least Tony Blair's vision of New Labour; his successor Gordon Brown, more of a Labour party traditionalist, never appeared to associate himself closely with Third Way politics. It was a distinctly 'Blairite' project (Naughtie 2003).

Anthony Giddens viewed the core principles of the Third Way as a valid and necessary response to the globalised, post-traditional '*runaway world*' in which social and economic realms were typified by uncertainty and risk (Giddens 1994: 3). He posited the need for a radical '*generative*' politics that must engage with this changed world – no longer structured by nature or tradition – to reform welfare systems to enable individuals to make meaningful, 'reflexive' choices by which they can successfully negotiate their own life course.

There were two core dimensions to the Third Way thesis. Firstly, it argued that the social and economic conditions that frame our lives had fundamentally changed. This analysis of the changes inherent in post-industrialism or post-Fordism underpinned much of New Labour's rhetoric and policy and were changes New Labour argued were inevitable and must be anticipated and accepted. For example: 'just as economic and social change were critical in sweeping the Right to power ... The challenge for the Third Way is to engage fully with the implications of that change' (Blair 1998: 6). He continued by identifying those changes as the 'growth in increasingly global markets and global culture,' 'technological advancement,' 'a transformation in the role of women' and 'radical changes in the nature of politics.' (1998: 6). Secondly, according to Giddens these changes rendered existing models of welfare obsolete or inadequate thus making reform essential. For example,

> Welfare reform should aim to achieve a new balance of risk and security in people's lives ... The post war welfare state was built around a passive notion of risk – and a passive notion of security ... We now live in much more risk active environments – an observation that stretches all the way from global markets through to family relations and health care systems. Welfare systems need to contribute to the entire spirit, encourage the resilience necessary to cope with a world of speeded up change, but provide security when things go wrong (Giddens 1998: 29).

Giddens argued for the importance of a 'social investment state', defined by a 'positive' welfare system that fosters in people a sense of personal responsibility to others and to the state, whilst resisting the temptation of top-down, 'negative' welfare that creates 'perverse consequences' such as dependency and social stagnation (Giddens 1998a: 113). This position was reflected in a distinction New Labour made between 'good' and 'bad' public expenditure whereby 'good' spending can be described as 'investment' – in education, job creation, childcare and more recently in children per se (Lister 2006); and 'bad' spending takes the form of unemployment benefit and generally the 'bills of economic and social failure'. As Blair explained: '... part of the budget is spending on pensions, child benefit and people with disabilities: good, we like that. The other part is spending on unemployment and people on benefit when they should be at work: bad, we want to decrease that' (cited in Powell 1999: 21). Whilst Giddens' theory of social change and his recommendations for welfare reform are central to his work, this derives from a concern with individuals and their relationship with the structures that govern their lives. For example, whilst his emphasis on 'positive' welfare is a response to the broad transformations that characterise the 'risk' (Beck 1992) or 'post-traditional' (Giddens 1994) society, the prescription for welfare reform is designed to promote the self-development of individual agents (McCullen and Harris 2004: 52) and enhance their ability to be effective social actors. Giddens strove for a diagnosis and prescription that would secure the symbiotic agency/ structure relationship. For Finlayson, Giddens' project was about 'redeveloping or repairing social cohesion and solidarity' (1999: 275).

Whilst Ulrich Beck argued that welfare must promote 'critical reflexivity' to negotiate risk (Deacon and Mann 1997), Giddens advocated the promotion, through welfare, of the 'autotelic self' – a normative model of individual consciousness that is more self-reliant and less contingent on certainty. His thesis rested on the belief that we now inhabit an insecure society, characterised by post-Fordist labour markets, changing family structures, widespread societal anxieties, increased scepticism about political authority (Kemshall 2002) and its ability to deliver social improvement (White 2001: xi). Crucially, Giddens differentiates this from 'traditional' society, which he correlates with Modernity. During that period, agents are said to have lived in a state of relative 'ontological security'. Human beings relationship with the external world was mediated by an attachment to certain traditions and customs, securing people in a reliable and consistent social context (Finlayson 1999: 276). Following this logic, for Giddens the transformation to a 'post-traditional' society and the implosion of traditions and security-inducing social structures had a knock-on effect for the individual sense of self, threatening to overwhelm our capacity to participate in social and economic systems. It is here that Giddens argues a Third Way can help. For Giddens these irrevocable changes required an assertive response that utilises the welfare state to assist individuals to cope with new and changed risks. What had now become a context of ontological *insecurity* required political strategies that enable individual agents to '… translate potential threats into rewarding challenges, someone who is able to turn entropy into a consistent flow of experience' (Giddens 1994: 192). He continues by defining the autotelic self as not seeking 'to neutralise risk or to suppose that "someone else will take care of the problem": risk is confronted as the active challenge which generates self-actualisation' (Giddens 1994: 192). It is by nurturing this kind of agency that the uncertainties of the transformed world could be negotiated and a sense of order could be maintained. Crucially, according to Giddens, a passive or overbearing welfare state cannot equip individuals with the necessary capacity to navigate life successfully.

New Labour's Welfare Settlement

The Third Way, as a doctrine for reinvigorating the politics of the centre-left, received significant criticism from both academic scholarship and political journalists.

Stuart Hall (1998) described the New Labour project as 'the great moving nowhere show' and argued how 'third way' politics shied away from radicalism, opting for a 'middle course' on everything. By 2001, *Guardian* journalist and sometime New Labour enthusiast Polly Toynbee proclaimed the 'third way' was 'utterly redundant' and 'an escape from self-definition – a butterfly always on the wing' because it 'offers the best of all possible worlds'. Paul Cammack went further and claimed: 'The "Third Way" reads not as an innocent manifesto for a resurgent centre left, but as a systematic appropriation of the vocabulary and values of social democracy to legitimise and consolidate a new politics of the Centre Right' (2004: 15). However, my point is not to dwell on the rights and wrongs of the Third Way's influence on New Labour, but rather to analyse how it fed into interesting developments in New Labour's welfare agenda. I want to explore two key aspects here. Firstly, what Giddens described as an 'active' welfare state was at the centre of New Labour's early welfare reform agenda, designed to forge a 'new welfare deal between the individual and the state' (Heron and Dwyer 1999: 91). In New Labour's first term in office, in the 1998 Green Paper, *New Ambitions for our Country: A New Contract for Welfare* (DSS 1998), Tony Blair outlined his vision of a modernised, Third Way style welfare state; not dismantled as favoured by neo-liberals, nor unreformed and therefore underperforming, but reformed on the basis of a new contract between the state and individual (Powell 1999). In reality, this tended to be translated into an increasingly conditional public welfare system underwritten by traditional assumptions of a culture of passivity and dependency amongst poor citizens. Then Chancellor of the Exchequer Gordon Brown commented:

> We must look hard at our own welfare system to ensure that it provides pathways out of unemployment and poverty rather than trapping people in persistent dependency. For the risks and insecurities that the welfare state was set up to combat have changed dramatically over fifty years and the welfare state has to keep up with the times. The welfare state must be about supporting people as they respond to these challenges – extending their choices and opportunities; acting as a trampoline rather than as a safety net (cited in Driver and Martell 1998: 107).

Similarly, Tony Blair identified what he considered the problems of a 'passive' welfare system: 'In addition, the way the welfare system works is encouraging dependency, reducing self-esteem and denying opportunity and responsibility in almost equal measure' (cited in Heron and Dwyer 1999: 100). In large part what was conceived as a 'new deal' brokered by an 'active' state tended to equate to a pretext for reconfiguring the contract between citizen and state along increasingly conditional lines, with access to social welfare increasingly dependent on citizens discharging prescribed 'responsibilities' (Dywer 1998: 493). New Labour's interpretation of Giddens' call for 'active welfare' and a self-directive citizen-sense tended to mean that those not in paid work or 'dependent' populations saw their access to welfare rights tightened further in the pursuit of welfare 'reform' and a 'work first' approach to poverty resolution (see Levitas 1998). In economic terms, the thrust of 'activation' policy was skewed towards those groups traditionally caught in the gaze of welfare 'reformers' – the poor, disabled people and lone parents. The Third Way became a rationale for those reforms; made rather more pernicious when framed by allusions to 'responsible' citizenship and the need to seize the opportunities generously bequeathed by this new incentivising, 'active' welfare state.

This brings me onto my second point about the Third Way. Whilst New Labour's 'new deal' centred around conditional welfare rights was clearly a central feature of the party's interpretation of 'active' welfare, it needs to be seen as part of a broader strategy for governing the social in which an overt politics of membership positioned citizens within particular civic and ethical formations replete with an array of social expectations; what Nikolas Rose usefully described as a 'grid of regulatory ideals' (1996: 145) shaping and infusing the performance of new citizenships. The responsibility to engage in paid employment was only one of an assemblage of moral imperatives that New Labour brought to bear on the individual in not only reforming the state welfare system, but in bolstering the civic community: reimagining the social through new narratives of personal and civic governance (Durose, Greasley and Richardson 2009: 1). In trying to understand the rationale and organisation of New Labour's strategy for the social, Stuart White (2001) has contended that the key organising principles of New Labour's re-tooling of the state – individual relationship were community, opportunity and responsibility. Indeed, Tony Blair argued that a reformed welfare state must be based on this triumvirate: '(it must) ... combine opportunity and responsibility as the foundation of community' (cited in Deacon 1998: 307). This formulation was an attempt to recast the welfare state as a generator of new societal relations and an inclusive, contingent citizenship. Here we have the other major contribution of the Third Way as Blair drew most heavily on its *spirit* of revisionism to transcend typical Left-Right political traditions and reconfigure contours of the social and the scope and meaning of the welfare state. It was important for Tony Blair and New Labour to attach themselves to a theory of social change and reform that would legitimise their claim of modernity and infuse their bid for transformative political power. The Third Way provided the most obvious intellectual texturing of that process. Looking back, it is arguable that the Third Way infused a spirit of modernising radical-centrism that sought to map out a social vision that rendered Labour Party shibboleths irrelevant whilst seeking reconciliation with laissez-faire capitalism – the two major strategic barriers to electoral success perceived by the party leadership.

In conclusion, having briefly given space to the Third Way and acknowledged its influence I am arguing that one can overplay its significance and should not give it undue prominence in the New Labour story. With this in mind we begin to turn away from it here and focus on the three principles identified by White which helped formulate and give expression to the 'modernised' social and welfare settlement that New Labour sought and the Third Way enabled. Examining some of these influences invites us to better understand how New Labour problematised and interpreted the social and political terrain it sought to govern with and through. The Third Way will always be inextricably linked to the New Labour project, but it is clear that in order to more fully understand the contours and objectives of that project we need to broaden our analytical horizons and unpack the key concepts.

New Labour and Community

Perhaps the key leitmotif of New Labour was its belief in, and commitment to community. This enthusiasm for community has been well documented (see for example, Driver and Martell 1997; Goes 2004; Levitas 2000; Heron 2001; Imrie and Raco 2004; Prideaux 2005; Worley 2005). It is generally considered New Labour's most notable attempt at a 'big idea' or narrative that symbolised its 'newness' (Goes 2004: 113) in addition to offering protection from criticism of being too closely associated with the market or the state (Fitzpatrick 2005a: 17). For example, Peter Mandelson and Roger Liddle stated in 1997 that New Labour's distinctive emphasis was 'its concept of community' which was not a 'soft and romantic concept', but a 'robust and powerful idea' which meant teamwork, mutuality and justice (cited in Goes 2004: 109). Tony Blair also pronounced:

> At the heart of my beliefs is the idea of community. I don't just mean the local villages, towns and cities in which we live. I mean that our fulfilment as individuals lies in a decent society of others. My argument ... is that the renewal of community is the answer to the challenges of a changing world (Blair cited in Levitas 2000: 189).

More recently, former Home Office Minister Hazel Blears wrote about her belief in 'community' wherein she asserted that it tends to be used, 'to mean what politicians want it to mean' and went onto note that,

> A more useful notion of community is a way of expressing fellowship, or a sense of belonging to one another in society. In a world of insecurity and globalisation, of a decline in trust and deference, this can be seen as more helpful and attractive. It is used as shorthand for the concept of the interdependence and mutuality of individuals and collections of people (Blears 2003: 9).

The use of community as New Labour's 'key collective abstraction' (Levitas 2000: 191) in both rhetoric and policy was noteworthy for its 'promiscuity' (Levitas 2000: 191) and took on both an abstract and concrete form. It was abstract in the sense illustrated by Blair and Blears above, in that there was a belief in a philosophical community that provides a collective pretext for all individual social action and underpins the liberal justice principle of exchanging rights and duties – what is termed 'fair reciprocity' (White 1999: 171). Indeed, for New Labour community appeared to be one of the few certainties in the new insecure, globalised social order. Furthermore, flowing from the existence of community as an *a priori* social fact was a normative framework constructing moral and behavioural parameters that manifest in a range of rights and responsibilities for community 'members'. For New Labour, community was the explicit governing discourse through which responsible citizens were (re)constituted (Clarke 2005) and their conduct was managed and could be challenged (Rose 2000). It is through the invoking of this model of community that New Labour articulated both a demand for responsible behaviour as well and claimed a commitment to the fair distribution of life opportunities through mild redistributions of wealth and investment in social infrastructure.

What we might consider to be a dynamic concept of community designed to reinvigorate the social contract and introduce an activist citizenship, was also deployed by New Labour as a form of 'metagovernance' that constituted binding 'narratives of collective meaning and identity' (Somerville 2005: 119). In this sense, references to community were a means of not only tethering individuals to collective norms, but of transcending class-based politics and unifying a fragmented and insecure polity. This analysis deems the appeal to community to be a response to perceived threats to social stability such as racialised fears of terrorism since 2001 (Craig 2007), the increase in economic migrants from EU accession countries since 2005 and the banking and recessionary crises of 2008. Gordon Brown's ascension to Prime Minister in 2007 was coupled with a concern to promote 'Britishness' as New Labour sought to reinforce a sense of a national 'public' (Newman and Clarke 2009). This was part of a longer legacy of concern about the cohesion and integrity of the social from New Labour – most evident in light of fears around the impact of multiculturalism (Worley 2005).

The Role of the Spatialised Community

The functioning of community as a philosophical precept and as a narrative of governance is complimented by New Labour's belief in the material importance of community as a socio-spatial entity. The transposing of community's ethical properties onto physical space was a feature of New Labour's social and urban policy. New Labour believed in the existence and positive role of spatial communities and was committed to both their physical refurbishment and their necessity as a behavioural framework. New Deal for Communities was the clearest policy expression of these commitments, although Lupton has noted that, rhetorically, New Labour usually favoured 'neighbourhood' as its 'key unit of policy delivery' (2003: 120). Nevertheless, the spatial community performed a crucial function for New Labour, what Raco and Imrie describe as 'a natural and desirable social formation, based on the diminution of difference and conflict, and the inculcation of shared values' (2003: 8). This is premised on the assumption that spatial proximity produces shared values and experiences, deriving from an assumed 'unitary sense of space' (Amin 2002: 972), which can and should be translated into a framework that provides the bedrock for civic renewal, social order and inclusion. For example, then Home Secretary Jack Straw pronounced in 2000, '... if you don't build strong and responsible communities then you end up with wastelands where there really is 'no such thing as society' (cited in Heron 2001). Moreover, the desire to 'build', 'empower' and 'strengthen' community (by which is meant actual collectives of people and families) is a manifestation of a Third Way concern with shoring up 'civil society' and reducing dependency on the state:

> The grievous twentieth century error of the fundamentalist Left was the belief that the state could replace civil society and thereby advance freedom ... A key challenge of progressive politics is to use the state as an enabling force, protecting effective communities and voluntary organisations and encouraging their growth (Blair 1998: 4).

Gordon Brown (2000a) perhaps conveyed the enthusiasm for a 'strong' civil society more clearly:

> This is my idea of Britain – because there is such a thing as society – community of communities, tens of thousands of local neighbourhood civic associations, unions, charity and voluntary organisations, each one unique and every one special. A Britain energised by a million centres of action and compassion, of concern and initiative that together embody a very British idea – that of civic society (http://www.hm-treasury.gov.uk/press_129_00.htm).

These representations of community may or may not reflect the entrenchment of neo-liberalism and the desire of government to offload the responsibilities of the state onto communities as suggested by Herbert (2005), but New Labour instituted a dedicated Department for Communities to manage its 'bewildering myriad of policies' (Imrie and Raco 2003) to promote civic engagement and 'community' self help. For example, Tony Blair stated a key goal of government is to, 'empower local communities to shape a better future for themselves' (SEU 1998). In addition, Hazel Blears wrote about putting 'communities in control' to create 'real public ownership' of services and decisions, which entails 'creating new forms of mutual governance' and 'shifting real power, opportunity – and responsibility – into the hands of working people' (2003: 15). 'Strong' communities were viewed as a bulwark against the uncertainties unleashed by globalisation whereby the state should no longer be relied upon to perform its protective role effectively. The state must be supported by 'empowered', self-governing 'communities' in which responsible citizenship is cultivated. This is consistent with Finlayson's analysis of Giddens' Third Way in which there is an ontological belief that power should not be concentrated in one centre, but dispersed amongst people and communities to encourage the reflexivity of citizens. The role of the state is a 'generative' one that facilitates this dispersal of power to the local and individual level (Finlayson 1999: 276). However, whilst New Labour emphasised acting responsibly and viewed citizen participation as a key to tackling social passivity, they did not advocate 'choice' and 'empowerment' in the name of individualism. Citizens were not to be cast adrift by the state to sink or swim, but were to remain anchored in a strong civic unit that both protected them from uncertainty and framed their behaviour. Community was meant to provide New Labour's 'autotelic' citizens with a sense of membership that shaped their 'freedom' to exercise 'choice' (Clarke 2005: 451).

New Labour and Responsibility

If community provided the guiding precept for a New Labour society, it was bolstered by an ethos of responsibility, which provided a 'regulatory ideal' for individual agency as well as a key goal for welfare reform. New Labour's normative social vision was one in which everyone knows the rules and contingent rights and responsibilities: 'The rights we enjoy reflect the duties we owe: rights and opportunity without responsibility are engines of selfishness and greed' (Blair 1998: 4). Also:

> Duty is the cornerstone of a decent society. It recognises more than self ... It draws on a broader and therefore more accurate notion of human nature than one formulated on insular self interest. The rights we receive should reflect the duties we owe. With the power should come responsibility (Blair 1995 cited Dwyer 1998: 499).

Therefore, 'responsibility' was part of the New Labour redefinition of the relationship between individual and state. This 'new contract' contained some key expectations of citizens and some welfare measures, including both incentives and sanctions, seen as necessary to uphold the contract and address the alleged dependency and passivity of some citizens. The emphasis on responsibility can be traced back to a Third Way notion of the welfare state as enabling and 'active', distributing 'equal opportunities' to equip individuals to meet and overcome the potential risks and insecurities of contemporary life. Responsible individual agents are central to this agenda as it is only they who can negotiate the pitfalls of modern life. As Giddens stated, 'Social democrats have to shift the relationship between risk and security involved in the welfare state, to develop a society of 'responsible risk takers' ... People need protection when things go wrong, but also the material and moral capabilities to move through major periods of transition in their lives' (1998b: 100).

Many critics such as Kemshall argue that such a focus on individual responsibility legitimises the withdrawal or retrenchment of state involvement in the provision of welfare as well as de-legitimise the claims of some groups to social welfare. Welfare claimants can be defined as 'unproductive' and 'scroungers' with no one but themselves to blame for their predicament (2002: 27). Indeed, in 2002 Tony Blair asserted, 'We shouldn't carry on paying out benefit to you in circumstances where you are not prepared to give anything back to society ... why should the state carry on paying out benefit to these people, subsidising their housing when they are using their housing to inflict misery on other people?' (Interview on *Newsnight*, 16 May). Deacon has noted that this was quite deliberate, as New Labour embraced an Americanisation of welfare in which increased attention was paid to the behaviour and morality of welfare claimants in response to conservative challenges from commentators such as Charles Murray, Larry Mead and others to take seriously issues of personal responsibility and social obligation (2000: 11). Moreover, implicit in their welfare reform agenda was a shift from thinking about inequality to thinking about welfare dependency (Deacon 2000: 16) and an associated concern with appearing 'tough' on those who are deemed to fail in meeting their obligations to the wider 'community' (Deacon 2004: 912).

David Marquand sought to locate New Labour's moralism (which its preoccupation with 'responsibility' and character could be said to illustrate) within a typology of political ideas since 1945 in the UK. He argued that Thatcherism was marked by a transformation from 'moral' to 'hedonistic' individualism during the mid-1980s as market forces failed to recreate moral order; a mutation that the New Right encouraged through tax cuts, easy credit and a consumer boom (1996: 26). The important insight of Marquand's analysis is that New Labour's rise to power is interpreted as a return to 'moral' collectivism. He argues that a similar moralist strand runs through post-war Beveridgean social democracy, (early) Thatcherism and Blairism (1996: 28). They all 'draw on the same reservoir of serious and sober virtues' (1996: 28). New Labour, then, can be said to have reinvigorated the moralist welfare tradition with an emphasis on imposing or incentivising 'good' behaviour. However, Marquand's analysis is undermined somewhat by New Labour's 'hedonistic' attitude to the reckless hubris of high finance and exorbitant quantities of consumer debt it allowed to accumulate. Nonetheless, New Labour's emphasis on a 'conduct of conduct' (Rose 1999) was operationalised on the basis of and through a politics of membership with community as its fulcrum (as demonstrated above). Hence, there was a need for policy measures that would facilitate and strengthen community whether through the encouraging of paid employment or specific behavioural codes such as civic participation. For New Labour therefore, the role of welfare was to mediate between individuals and the community, ensuring that rights were fairly allocated (constituting community) and responsibilities fulfilled (preserving community). Often this involved challenging and changing the character and behaviour of community 'members'. This tended to manifest most visibly not just in addressing alleged cultures of welfare 'dependency' and non-employment, but of citizen apathy and 'yobbishness' and general 'antisocial' behaviour.

The main influences on New Labour's thinking on character, welfare and behaviour have been identified as Christian socialism, new communitarianism

(Deacon 2002b: 115; Deacon and Mann 1997) and the 'new paternalism' of Mead and others (White, S. 2003: 12).[4] The Third Way is also a key influence here as Driver has noted, 'New Labour welfare reforms demand, as the new paternalism requires, certain types of behavioural response and sanction those forms of behaviour deemed "irresponsible". Third Way politics is not neutral on the "good citizen"' (2004: 35). New Labour's 'good citizen' was not just one who was self sufficient and took up paid employment, or did not sap the resources of the state, but was someone who fulfilled a range of civic responsibilities with appropriate moral rectitude. Not only were they forthright on the responsibility of people to take paid work, they introduced a variety of initiatives, designed to shape an ideal moral community. The most high profile incarnation of these was the Respect Action Plan, launched in 2006 and containing a range of measures designed to address 'bad' behaviour and provide state support for people and families who require help in developing appropriate behaviour patterns.[5] In his foreword to the document, Tony Blair reiterated the New Labour analysis of 'community' and those who threaten it:

> But there are still intractable problems with the behaviour of some individuals and families, behaviour which can make life a misery for others, particularly those in the most disadvantaged communities. What lies at the heart of this behaviour is a lack of respect for values that almost everyone in this country shares – consideration for others, a recognition that we all have responsibilities as well as rights, civility and good manners (Respect Task Force 2006: 1).

The other key influence on Tony Blair was the philosophy of John Macmurray whom he encountered whilst at Oxford University. The influence of Macmurray on the Blair philosophy has been discussed at length elsewhere (See, for example, Prideaux 2005), but it was Macmurray's views on 'community' that appears to have appealed to Blair. Whilst Blair did not follow Macmurray's eschewing of organised politics, the notion of a community, believed to go deeper than any kind of organised society, was said to have stayed with him (Naughtie 2002: 20). As noted above, this vision of community bore close similarity to that envisaged by new communitarianism.[6]

---

4   The rise of the issue of antisocial behaviour in policy thinking has complex roots, separate from much of the general thinking on welfare and character, but sharing some of the same suspicions of '1960s liberalism' (Blair 2004) that communitarians have expressed. See Squires (2006) for an introduction to these roots.

5   The launching of this agenda appears to have been about more than policy details, which as many commentators have noted had been introduced or mooted before, and was actually about attempting to map out a moral vision of the 'community' and disseminate this vision via the media.

6   The influence of new communitarianism on New Labour has been noted by several authors (for example, Driver and Martell 1998; Dwyer and Heron 1999; Levitas 2000; Prideaux 2005).

Amitai Etzioni – the leading exponent of new communitarianism – argued that it was an attempt to reassert social and moral order in response to the excessive individualism and' rights based' culture of the 1980s and 1990s entailing a need for a 'new golden rule': 'Respect and uphold society's moral order as you would have society respect and uphold your autonomy' (1997: xviii). New communitarians advocated measures to strengthen social order and communal solidarity, whilst tethering an individual's freedom to their responsibility to the wider community in which they live and flourish. They sought to reinvigorate a moralist strand of liberal thought which sailed too closely to conservative winds for some (see Prideaux 2001).

Nonetheless, New Labour seized upon this moment and embraced the 'return of the agent' (Deacon and Mann 1999: 423). Alan Deacon reinforces this view, arguing that New Labour engaged with ideas of character and behaviour to break with the 'excessive structuralism and determinism' that characterised much of centre Left thinking in the UK and USA on welfare for much of the post war period (2002a: 182).[7] Hence, both New Labour and the New Democrats strove to tackle welfare dependency and get 'tough on crime' or bad behaviour, framing it in new communitarian language about behaviour and 'responsibility' to the 'community'. Etzioni stated (in language one suspects Tony Blair was always straining to adopt):

> We must all live with the consequences of children who are not brought up properly, whether bad economic conditions or self-centred parents are to blame. Juvenile delinquents … mug the elderly, hold up stores and gas stations, and prey on innocent children returning from school. They grow up to be useless, or worse, employees, and they can drain taxpayers' resources and patience … Therefore, parents have a moral responsibility to the community to invest themselves in the proper upbringing of their children, and communities – to enable parents to so dedicate themselves (1993: 54).

Echoing Etzioni, New Labour's vision of responsible citizenship extended beyond paid work and encroached upon 'private' realms of home and family and was comfortable about forming judgements about individual behaviour (Clarke 2005) in a way the Party had perhaps not been for several years.

Another influence on this agenda was James Q. Wilson's (1993) analysis of a corrosive 'spirit of the age' which, Wilson argued, encouraged a relativistic respect for moral 'diversity' and 'difference' which undermined behavioural norms and constrained the ability of the community to form judgements about the values and choices made by its individual members. In response, Wilson advocated the rediscovery of our 'moral sense' through which positive social norms could be

---

7   Fitzpatrick (2005b) offers a challenge to Deacon's analysis of the 'quasi-Titmuss' paradigm arguing that the focus of Leftist welfare debates has been on contextualising individual behaviour as opposed to ignoring it.

reclaimed. New Labour propounded a social vision which resonated with Wilson's belief in this inherent, universal 'moral sense' that citizens and governments must embrace. Communities therefore are nothing less than embodiments of 'our' intuitive but evolved sense of right and wrong whilst pretending that there are acceptable variations of morality and rules governing conduct is a betrayal of 'our' natural intuition. The outcome is a strict conception of behavioural parameters and an unswerving belief in forming judgements of those who deviate. We saw the influence of this thinking in New Labour's attempts to mark out the boundaries of acceptable behaviour and construct deviance as a form of disobedience from what is naturally and self-evidently 'right' to the 'decent' mainstream – a distinction that became a depressing mantra of New Labour politicians. The belief in community both as a national collective and as a local unit of social life was – in part – a means of articulating this behavioural settlement and often the material site at which this settlement was enforced. Documents such as the Respect Action Plan shared Wilson's view of the need to: 'recover the confidence with which [people] once spoke about virtue and morality...[and] to re-establish the possibility and the reasonableness of speaking frankly and convincingly about moral choices' (1993: vii, brackets added). In policy terms, irresponsible parents, antisocial young people, 'nightmare neighbours', truant schoolchildren, binge drinkers, public smokers, squeegee merchants, street beggars and the obese were a few groups who fell foul of this moralising settlement and were all deemed to have transgressed the 'norms' of the community at some point under New Labour Governments. A useful example of the mobilisation of community came when Tony Blair spoke about recasting the criminal justice system and putting the 'decent, law abiding majority in charge' (Blair cited in Squires and Stephen 2005: 522). This tended to manifest in 'community enforcement' processes, which in theory meant a role for 'good' citizens in defining punishments for deviant behaviour (for example. in public 'naming and shaming' campaigns for ASBO recipients) or receiving reparations from the deviant in the form of initiatives such as 'Community Payback' (Respect Task Force 2006: 35).[8] In addition, Former Home Secretary David Blunkett advocated the role of community groups in the prosecution and punishment of antisocial offenders. He argued that the Crown Prosecution Service should be more engaged with local communities to find out who should be fast tracked to court. The involvement of local 'communities' in the policing of offenders and defining offending was a communitarian-type approach that treated the 'community' as a moral agent whose values should be enforced to promote order and social cohesion. It was also seen as intrinsic to the alleged 'empowerment' of such social groupings whereby they have the power to identify deviants in their midst and ensure 'community safety' (Prior 2005).

---

8   A national project, launched in 2005 that makes 'unpaid work by offenders visible and promotes the engagement of local communities in selecting the work to be done by offenders' (Respect Task Force 2006: 35). This agenda also formed a key plank of New Labour's 2010 general election manifesto.

By contrast, John Clarke suggested that New Labour's ideal citizens were 'moralised, choice making, self-directing subjects' which were not just 'responsible', but the product of 'responsibilisation' whereby the 'citizen' had been (re)constituted as a 'self regulating subject' through frames or discourses of 'responsible' behaviour 'across a variety of sites and practices from teenage pregnancy, through the etiquette of summoning ambulances, to clearing up your dog's faeces' (Clarke 2005: 451–2). Therefore, New Labour's welfare regime can be viewed as helping construct the brand of community it desired through individual 'responsibilisation' in which rules and norms circulated the public domain and (they hoped) penetrated private spheres. This is an impulse of advanced-liberal governmentality (see Dean 1999) in which the individual and the civic are bound together by a rationality of de-centred government where the social becomes key terrain for (re)producing self-governing subjects. There is a resemblance here with Etzioni's (1997) 'moral voice' where conduct is shaped by both the inculcation of a loud and consistent inner personal voice bolstered by a strong external or communal voice (Deacon 2002b: 71).

Beyond public discourses of 'good' behaviour designed to nurture that 'moral voice', there were a concrete range of powers at the disposal of welfare managers designed to compel or persuade people to act in 'responsible' ways. These included benefit sanctions for parents of truant school pupils, curfews, anti-social behaviour orders (ASBOs), fixed penalty fines for 'yobbish' behaviour, rules for council house tenants that set out 'appropriate' behaviour, probationary tenancy periods and parenting classes. Whether we were children, parents, pupils, employees or service users, New Labour located our behaviour within the community and was unafraid to mobilise it to challenge or eradicate any behaviour it deemed to have transgressed its parameters. This firming up of norms and expectations was a fluid, symbiotic process meant to produce both moral cohesion and model citizenship and owed as much to New Labour's moralising sense as well as the governmentality of advanced liberalism.

In sum, New Labour sought to reinvigorate a moralising welfare agenda based on a communitarian-type vision of social order, shared moral values and a re-tooled welfare state that was an 'explicit mechanism for moral regeneration' (Deacon and Mann 1999: 426). This was fused with a 'third way' desire to '(re)constitute' individual social agents as 'reflexive' and 'responsible' citizens within this collective framework. In order to achieve this, they sought to 'responsibilise' and introduced a range of welfare measures designed to encourage, condition or impose behavioural codes or responsibilities seen as necessary for the brand of community and individual agency required. Underpinning this approach was a belief in the need to re-assert the 'moral sense' (Wilson 1993) because it offered certainty in forming moral judgements and could liberate the 'decent' majority who were in touch with this sense. New Labour politicians often viewed themselves as being at the vanguard of this struggle over moral choices and Tony Blair in particular appeared at his most confident when patrolling this divide.

These two objectives merged when New Labour sought to put the consensual, 'respectable' law abiding majority who *are* the community in charge of regulating the behaviour of a presupposed deviant and antisocial minority of individuals who are deemed to need it. This is seen most clearly in 'community enforcement' measures designed to mobilise the (supposedly unified) voice of the majority to police or manage deviant 'others' be they ASBO recipients, 'nuisance' neighbours or benefit 'cheats'. New Labour's community had behavioural and moral parameters that determined entry and membership and was deployed to cultivate responsible citizenship as well as police, moralise and reconstruct the 'problematic' minority. They defined some behaviour that went against these parameters as intrinsically anti-social and requiring 'tough' action since it represents a 'thoroughgoing debasement of community and civic culture itself ... a profound moral challenge to a broad consensus of accepted values' (Squires 2006: 149). To an extent therefore, community was used to 'identify New Labour's enemies' (Levitas 1998: 122), which Mandelson and Liddle (1996) defined as, 'the inefficient who let the community down and impede its success' and 'the irresponsible who fall down on their obligations to their families and therefore their community' (cited in Levitas 1998: 122). New Labour believed it has uncovered the correct language by which to assert those obligations and why they must be defended.

Ultimately, at the root of New Labour's welfare agenda was a desire to create, 'a social order in which people behaved differently rather than one in which resources are distributed differently' (Deacon 1998: 306). New Labour citizens were both 'actuarial subjects' who 'understand themselves as responsible and independent agents' (Clarke 2005: 452) and members of a community which defines their responsibilities to themselves and others. It also returns us to the 'third way' 'active' welfare state that does not seek to significantly redistribute wealth, or regulate the market but seeks to change the behaviour of people to negotiate and profit from the market on their own terms. It is also a welfare system that challenges the alleged dependency and passivity of some citizens by encouraging or compelling them to not only seek paid employment, but to participate in their communities and 'partner' the state in improving the delivery of public services and reproduce social order.

The flip side of New Labour's responsibility agenda and its priorities of paid employment, civic engagement, good parenting and well-behaved young people – was a concern to allocate opportunities to the members of its 'community'. It is to these that we now turn.

New Labour and Opportunity

Much has been made so far about the importance New Labour attached to behaviour and character and the role welfare can play in shaping these. However, it would be unfair to convey that that was the sum of their welfare reform agenda. The existence of structural poverty and social exclusion may not have been spoken about too often in public, but it is clear that New Labour accepted their existence, and that acceptance shaped their welfare agenda to some degree (Deacon 2003). Therefore, New Labour's welfare state was one that shaped behaviour, but also sought to offer 'protection' and opportunity for its citizens. Gordon Brown spoke about the necessity of providing opportunities:

> So we must create a country where there are new opportunities for everyone – millions of points of opportunity ... And I make no apologies for saying government has a responsibility in creating this new ladder of opportunity ... That will allow many, by their own efforts, to benefit from the opportunities once open only to a few (cited in Levitas 1998: 156).

New Labour governments undertook influential studies that identified and publicised the key dimensions of poverty. For example, the 2002 Department for Work and Pensions report *Opportunity for All*, contained a description of these dimensions: lack of resources, lack of opportunities to work or learn, health inequalities, lack of decent housing, disruption of family life and living in a disadvantaged neighbourhood (2002: 16). There was also some belief that poverty is transmitted from one generation to the next and that some groups are more likely to suffer – women, minority ethnic groups, pensioners, disabled people and people from large families (2002: 21). In this context, New Labour's focus on paid work was rooted in the belief that it offered the best protection from poverty and social exclusion, not just that it is a moral and social good. To some degree, New Labour attempted to balance protection for people from poverty through welfare to work and tax credits and avoiding perpetuating a passive welfare system that they argued would condemn people to dependency. As noted above, Deacon (2003) suggested that their response to this balancing act was to both 'level the playing field' and 'activate the players'. The main way in which they tried to level the playing field was by breaking cycles of disadvantage that were said to reproduce inequalities over time and generations. The 'cycle of deprivation' was the analytical base of New Labour's understanding of poverty and at the root of their commitment to eradicate child poverty within a generation (Deacon 2003). Gordon Brown (1999), who was reportedly keen to pursue a reputation of being something of a champion of the poor (Naughtie 2002: 269) emphasised the importance of breaking these cycles:

> We know that children who grow up in poor families are less likely to reach their full potential, less likely to stay on at school, or even attend school, more likely to fall into to dead end unemployment and poverty as an adult, more likely to become teenage mothers, more likely to be in the worst jobs or no jobs at all, more likely to be trapped in a no-win situation – poor when young, unemployed when older (http://archive.treasury.gov.uk/speech/cx70799.html).

Opportunity for All identified three ways in which poverty can be transmitted: children can be born poor and stay poor (through parental worklessness, low income and ill health); children can 'inherit' poverty (by doing poorly at school the same as their own parents); and poverty can be transmitted by locality and the poor services in that area (DWP 2002: 92).

A 2001 Treasury report on tackling child poverty also attempted to explain the process of poverty transmission through a framework beginning with low family or household income. This can cause two sources of disadvantage: parenting problems or a lack of role models within the family as well as living with spatial deprivation which can then lead to a severe reduction in life chances (HM Treasury 2001a: 16). This report focused on the structural impacts on child poverty and there was no mention of behaviour or agency (or measures to improve these), except where it concerns parents. New Labour identified the role that 'bad' parenting can play in reducing life chances and transmitting poverty and took steps through Sure Start and parenting orders to address this. Whilst many, including Ruth Levitas (1998) criticised New Labour for privileging paid work over unpaid care work, Driver and Martell (2002) argued that New Labour did value unpaid parenting work, not always in economic terms, but in terms such as morality, responsibility, security and children's opportunities (2002: 216).

Deacon (2002a) argued that any mention of behaviour by New Labour, in the context of poverty transmission, was presented as a response to or adaptation to adverse circumstances. That is, they did not accept a purely structural explanation of the transmission of disadvantage which denied the role of agency. They did emphasise structural factors, as they are central to the problem, but their analysis of agency tended to be 'adaptive' in that they suggested that behaviour plays a small role in perpetuating the cycle of deprivation, but only in response to their structural conditions (Deacon 2003: 133), hence their concern with parenting. They acknowledged that living in poverty can severely disrupt family life and present problems when raising children. Where New Labour differ from the 'adaptive' account of the cycle of disadvantage (see Wilson 1987) New Labour appeared to claim that the creation of more opportunities in education and employment is not enough; steps had to be taken to ensure the poor or workless were persuaded, encouraged or compelled to take those opportunities. This is what they considered 'activating the players' to mean in creating a truly effective anti-poverty strategy.

New Labour recognised that addressing structural inequalities was vital if efforts towards a more meritocratic society with genuine 'opportunities for all' were to be realised (Blair 1998). The desire to enhance the asset base of poor children through measures like the child trust fund was based on this recognition. Tony Blair wrote about the scheme at the time:

> Those benefits are not extended through society. Too many children are excluded from life chances before they are born because of poverty. They are forced to leave school at 16, not 18, to begin earning. They lack the capital to pay deposits or stamp duty on a first home. They are daunted by the prospect of going to university. Their ambitions are diminished at an early age. They lack the wealth that is the springboard of opportunity ... Overcoming the inequalities of wealth

and income that hold people back is one the greatest challenges facing Britain (Blair 2003).

Overall, New Labour exhibited a clear recognition of the need to protect citizens, especially children, from poverty, primarily by breaking cycles of deprivation. From New Labour's perspective, this meant introducing a variety of policy interventions designed to create more and better opportunities for the poorest and tackle the factors they identified as reinforcing their disadvantage.

New Labour and Social Exclusion

Labour's anti-poverty strategy was underpinned by the concept of social exclusion, a strategy that received a high profile from the beginning of the Blair administration, symbolised by the setting up of the Social Exclusion Unit (SEU) within the Cabinet Office in 1998. Peter Mandelson defined social exclusion, not unproblematically in 1997, thus: 'This is about more than poverty and unemployment. It is about being cut off from what the rest of us regard as normal life. It is called social exclusion, what others call the "underclass"' (1997: 1). A slightly more subtle definition was offered by the SEU: '... shorthand term for what can happen when people or areas suffer from a combination of linked problems such as unemployment, poor skills, low incomes, poor housing, high crime, bad health and family breakdown' (SEU 2001b). New Labour saw social exclusion as being more than income inequality, but the destination that people, families or communities reach if they are not helped to overcome cyclical processes of poverty, lack of skills, poor education and generally substandard public services. Social exclusion was measured at one stage by over 50 government indicators (Alcock 2004: 88), indicating the breadth of factors believed can exacerbate or precipitate this condition. As exclusion became the focus of government social policy, there were efforts to understand the causes, identify those most 'at risk' and outline the financial and human costs of this social division. This culminated in a range of interventions, introduced by government and designed to re-attach the excluded to the 'mainstream of society'. Three policy strategies for combating exclusion were set out (SEU 2001b):

- *Prevention*: In-work tax credits, New Deal welfare to work programmes, Sure Start childcare centres, crime reduction partnerships, improving quality of local authority care.
- *Reintegration*: adult basic skills courses, Drug Testing and Treatment Orders (DTTO), Rough Sleepers Unit, New Deal for Communities.
- *Ensuring basic minimum standards*: floor targets for local authority services, out of school education for excluded children, improving NHS services and access.

These are just some of the measures introduced to address the dynamics of social exclusion, as analysed by New Labour. They imply that policy interventions were viewed as being able to prevent some 'at risk' groups arriving at an excluded destination, and hope that other measures can re-integrate and retrieve those already experiencing such conditions.

The belief that policy initiatives could 're-integrate' appears to include a degree of prescription for changing the behaviour of the excluded. That is, in addition to targeted support and extra resources, there was a strain running through programmes like the Drug Treatment and Testing Orders and NDC that was explicitly aimed at facilitating (or compelling) different modes of behaviour. Chapter 3 will explore this in more detail and will unpack how NDC was constituted as a means of re-attaching excluded individuals and communities through investment in neighbourhood infrastructure and transformations in the culture of the local-social. How New Labour attempted to 'include' and 'reintegrate' the residents of excluded communities is a key concern for this discussion and so the next chapter will examine how NDC was organised in order to achieve this end.

Conclusion

The purpose of this chapter has been to map out some of the political, intellectual and philosophical backdrop to the NDC programme which is the focus of our discussion here. By locating the NDC within a wider welfare agenda, it is possible to identify how New Labour constructed its neighbourhood regeneration approach as both an ethical project designed to transform individual behaviour and neighbourhood culture, whilst providing opportunities for local residents to participate in the governance of their locale. The next chapter moves on to situate NDC within a different policy dynamic which New Labour engaged with and interpreted to some degree: the creation of dispersed sites of governance which draw in 'communities' as participatory entities involved in their own management and regeneration as well as unsettling established means of designing and delivering welfare. The interplay between New Labour's welfare agenda and this policy dynamic are explored by way of introducing and unpacking NDC in more detail.

Chapter 3

Local Governance and New Deal
for Communities

Introduction

Having explored in the previous chapter what is considered here as the distinctive approach of the New Labour governments to tackling social exclusion within a broader project for governing and reimagining the social, this chapter begins with an examination of some of the continuities in social and urban policy that contextualise New Labour's endeavours. Chapter 2 consisted of an exposition of New Labour thinking around three key concepts of community, responsibility and opportunity and used an examination of these concepts to start to move from a discussion of New Labour's wider strategies for welfare to focus on the specific policy area under scrutiny here – the regeneration of poor or 'excluded' neighbourhoods. This chapter continues this process, but rather than focusing on New Labour thinking per se, it does so through a discussion of developments in the role and scope of the state that shape the social and urban policy realities that somewhat transcend the New Labour era. Chapter 2 touched on the need to acknowledge that approaches to reforming the welfare state and the reconfiguring of individual citizenship can have origins external to any political project or movement. Therefore, it is important to acknowledge that social and urban policy under New Labour was not simply a manifestation of Third Way theory or the moral proclivities of politicians, but was an engagement with, and negotiation of prevailing shifts in the scope and meaning of government, recalibrations of the welfare state and contingent policy logics. Indeed, we must be wary of assuming a coherent, constructive engagement between politics and broader shifts in economic, social and political structures. A more nuanced analysis needs to point to the unstable and fluid relationship between the technologies of politics and the terrain it seeks to map and manage. This chapter therefore, seeks to explore some of the exogenous influences on the shifts and transformations in the scope of the state, the meaning of citizenship and the terrain of the social that occurred during New Labour's time in office. This is an important contribution to my analysis of how and why New Labour sought the regeneration of excluded socio-spatial territories. Afterwards, the chapter moves on to discuss the NDC programme directly and unpack its main conceptual and practical components. We can do this having set out both the political and policy contexts in which this programme was embedded, progressing to draw out the key dynamics which underpin it. Finally, the chapter moves on to provide some background to the fieldwork undertaken in an NDC neighbourhood which is used to inform discussions in subsequent chapters.

The Shift to Governance?

We can partly interpret the 'reimaginings' and new governing strategies of New Labour and the Third Way as responses to the growing social complexity, fragmentation and insecurity wrought by shifts in cultural and economic spheres which have unsettled or undermined the traditional modalities of the sovereign state (see Rose 1999). This climate of uncertainty or risk (Beck 1992) has, suggest some scholars, led to a shift from government to governance in which there is a recalibration of the role and standing of the state and new sets of relationships are forged with markets and civil society in sustaining social development (Kooiman 1999; Stoker 2000). This is often analysed as an epochal change signifying the rescaling of government from a hierarchical and unitary system of control towards greater devolution, decentralisation and dispersal of power and resources to a plurality of sub-national and/or non-state actors (see Swyngedouw 2005; Taylor 2007). An important aspect of the alleged shift from government to governance is that it relies upon an active and engaged public sphere as a 'partner' in directing and implementing policy (Barnes et al. 2003) and in 're-inventing government' (Newman and Clarke 2009: 49). Furthermore, public participation is often framed in spatial terms, drawing in neighbourhoods, communities and resident citizens as key actors in circuits of self-governance that operate through shared geographic and institutional spaces. Spatialised localities such as neighbourhoods are recruited into policymaking spheres of influence and constructed as participants in the generation and direction of their own trajectories (Lowndes and Sullivan 2008) and stand in counterpoint and as an important corrective to the alleged excesses of both state and market. These socio-spatial entities are constructed as consensual and generative partners, assumed to contribute to a shared political agenda in which both the central and local come together, to pursue (under a New Labour government) a Third Way or 'one nation' project of economic prosperity and social justice (Davies 2005) and what Newman (2001: 142) calls 'a new social settlement' in which there is a transition in civic relations and the regeneration of ethical citizenship (Wallace 2009). There is some disagreement about the extent to which we have moved into an era of dispersed governance (see Davies 2005), but it is the case that in recent years we have seen growing debates around the 'inviting' of individuals and neighbourhoods into the policy gaze (Swyngedouw 2005; Taylor 2007; Amin 2005) as part of a territorialising of the social into governable, spatially-bounded sites which function as partners in the production of public policy (Wallace 2010). Whilst, the desire to widen citizen participation in policymaking and implementation is not a new phenomenon (see John 2009), latterly there has been a hardening in political terms which has found expression in concepts like 'double devolution' (Miliband 2006), 'new localism' (ODPM 2005) and a growing desire to place 'communities in control' (DCLG 2008a). Similarly, the Conservative Party under David Cameron has spoken about the need for a 'big society' in a 'post-bureaucratic age' with an emphasis on local autonomy which can revitalise the civic and challenge the alleged institutional and cultural dominance of the state (see for example, 2009).

A further important development in the rearticulating of the state and social is said to be a 'remapping' of the public (Newman and Clarke 2009) in which new selfhoods and new relationships are generated through situated citizenships framed by a politics of membership that more closely defined norms of individual conduct. This is in response to crises of cohesion and the need to accommodate difference within the public domain, resulting in a turn to a governing language of 'community' (Newman and Clarke 2009: 44). For Bauman, this 're-rooting' of the self occurs within a 'postulated moral community' which has implications for the 'autonomous moral responsibility' of individuals (1993: 46), but for New Labour, it was important to try and embed and frame citizenship through community, partly out of an ethical belief in the virtues inherent in living with a collective sense, partly in order to moralise problematic individuals and families and partly out of a desire to protect citizens from a fragmented social and anchor them in a more consistent, secure local lifeworld. However, in a wider sense embedding citizenship in community can also be viewed as part of an instrumental rearticulation of the state in light of shifts in the meaning and scope of sovereign political government; it became important to secure the participation of citizens in governing projects both in terms of a national public (Newman and Clarke 2009) and the local–social.

Theorising governance in this manner invites us to consider that the NDC programme can be interpreted as an example of a welfare programme infused with New Labour-driven preoccupations and objectives but framed by a logic of governance that necessitates the 'partnering' and 'empowering' of local communities whilst helping bind citizens in solidary social units. This is a concomitant of the decentring of the state. However, there are some important rejoinders to what can sometimes appear in the literature to be an inexorable and unproblematic drive towards a networked, pluralistic governing model and 'empowerment' agenda. For example, it is clear that the NDC programme did not involve a wholesale devolution or dispersal of power to the local community. In fact, what is important to note here is that the shift-to-governance narrative has revealed an unstable assemblage of governing projects involving an interplay of decentralisation rhetoric, new sites of 'respatialised' welfare (Daly 2003), new opportunities for citizen engagement alongside a tightening of performance management systems and centralised targeting (Durose, Creasley and Richardson 2009: 5) and increased surveillance by the central state. These tensions and contradictions unsettle both the tendency towards a simplistic reading of governance scales from local to supranational, each fitting neatly into the other (Newman and Clarke 2009) and invite us to consider the experiences of citizens 'invited' to negotiate new governance spaces (Taylor 2007). New Labour (like their political descendants David Cameron and the 'New Tories') was guilty of propounding an unproblematic localising impulse, presenting 'active citizenship' and 'empowered communities' as self-evident social goods. Further, what is interesting about such policy discourses is how they simultaneously create and close down modalities of power, ensnaring (often disadvantaged) citizens in complex spaces they must contend with and manage. This locates the empowered citizen/community – through which governance is valorised – within difficult terrain in which autonomy can be both enhanced but mediated through new matrices of control. With this in mind, it is worth noting Daly's critique of governance as 'state-centred' and tending to 'frame change ... in terms of a rearticulation of the state rather than originating in society' (2003: 125). This is not a view I wholly share (see Wallace 2009), but it is one which usefully reminds us that governance and the concomitant recruiting of 'active' territories and individuals in reproducing government should not be interpreted purely as a response to exogenous risks originating at a geopolitical level, or to a crisis of sovereign bureaucratic government (Rhodes 1996). In fact, there is a fluid relationship between forms of governance and the social, particularly as interpreted and instituted by New Labour. For example, we can, in part, situate recent assumptions of co-operative, co-producing civic territories within an idealised reading of civic forms such as community and their ability to ameliorate the sterility of state-driven social development. In other words, the assumed (or mythologised) properties and dynamics of 'organic' civic space have been incorporated into the reframing of welfare practice which has been infused by particular representations of communities – if provided with appropriate support – as consensual, strong and entrepreneurial (Newman and Clarke 2009; Wallace 2009). Furthermore, there has been an interpretation of political and cultural struggles for citizen rights that has infused the shift towards partnership governance. To some extent, the partnership governance model as conceived by New Labour is framed partly by a calculation that citizens have proven over time that they want greater control over their lives and will disrupt 'traditional' governing practices to achieve it (see John 2009). Therefore, New Labour believed it could and should provide opportunities for individual and collective self-help and expression. For example,

> Our history is punctuated by great struggles for democracy ... the Rochdale families who took control over the food they bought by creating the first co-operative ... to the Chartists who marched in their thousands at Kersal Moor ... Ours is a government committed to greater democracy, devolution and control for communities. We want to see stronger local councils, more co-operatives ... more people becoming active in their communities as volunteers, advocates and elected representatives (Blears 2008: iii).

If we consider this indicative, the contours and meanings of governance and 'post-bureaucratic' citizenship are infused to some extent by a powerful narrative of popular civic activism and the active community. The increased emphasis by policymakers on citizen participation derives not only from the experience of 'failed', unresponsive policies, but from a desire to incorporate citizen voices within the fabric of policy itself. The notion of an active citizenry was and continues to be appropriated and internalised by new governance strategies that transform citizens into 'partners' and 'stakeholders'. These constituent narratives of governing through the social and through community further problematise how citizens respond to government-sponsored projects of autonomy. Under New Labour, participation was constructed not only as an opportunity but largely as an obligatory responsibility which partly underpinned its contractualist citizenship and regenerative civic vision. The scope of 'legitimate' resistance to these projects is delimited by the fact that citizen participation is situated in a consensual and restorative model of community and constructed as an internalised, magnanimous response to a legacy of activism. How citizens respond and react to a policy framework which celebrates and even *expects* individual and community agency is a key problematic in my analysis of local citizen governance and it is in this complex terrain that we can situate NDC and start to problematise its meaning and impact.

Introducing NDC

Having located NDC within New Labour's welfare reform agenda designed to offer both opportunity and protection to its citizens or 'community' members and nurture, persuade or compel certain kinds of behaviour in those same members as well as a shifting policy terrain wrought by a decentring of state planning, I want now to focus on and start to unpack NDC and explore the genesis, structure and objectives of the programme. NDC, as part of New Labour's Neighbourhood Renewal agenda giving added impetus to the 'urban question' (Lawless et al. 2009) was explicitly concerned with addressing social exclusion (Foley and Martin 2000) and grew out of the SEU's concerns with 'problem estates' (Alcock 2004) and a belief that area based initiatives (ABI's) would be the most effective response (Alcock 2004: 88). NDC was conceived as a regeneration programme designed to 'renew' socially excluded spaces by delivering resources to the local level and empowering local residents to affect long term change in their communities. It was part of New Labour's identification of: 'the increasing polarisation between thriving communities on the one hand, and deprived ones on the other ... over the past 20 years' (DSS 1999, cited in Hills and Stewart 2005) and was introduced by New Labour to tackle: 'the unacceptably bad conditions in this country's poorest neighbourhoods' (SEU 2001a).

As we saw in Chapter 1, the tackling of spatially concentrated urban poverty has been a feature of British public policy since at least the 1960s (Cochrane 2000; Lupton 2003; Lupton and Power 2005). New Labour were clear that they believed locality could play a significant part in perpetuating cycles of deprivation and that social exclusion could be spatial as well as afflicting individuals or families (SEU 2001b). Tony Blair conveyed his impression of the problems of these areas:

'We all know the problems of our poorest neighbourhoods – decaying housing, unemployment, street crime and drugs. People who can, move out. Nightmare neighbours move in. Shops and banks and other vital services close' (cited in SEU 1998). In 1998, the Social Exclusion Unit identified up to 4,000 neighbourhoods which were not only poor, but which were: 'pockets of intense deprivation where the problems of unemployment and crime are acute and hopelessly tangled up with poor health, housing and education. They have become no-go areas for some and no-exit zones for others' (SEU 1998: 9). This report stated that in the 10 per cent most deprived wards in 1998, 44 per cent of residents were receiving means-tested benefits compared to a 22 per cent national average. There were also 43 per cent of homes 'not in a decent state', compared with 29 per cent elsewhere, as well as more family 'breakdown', increasing availability of illegal drugs and an increased concentration of vulnerable people (SEU 2001a: 12). Through NDC the New Labour government set aside £2 billion for the 39 most deprived neighbourhoods in England (measured according to the Index of Multiple Deprivation). They made clear that 'communities' should be at the heart of the partnerships formed by local agencies (public, business and voluntary sectors), and special efforts should be made to engage hard-to-reach groups in consultation processes (NRU 2001: 11). The partnerships had to identify the needs of a given area and formulate a delivery plan and submit it to central government. If plans were approved, implementation procedures could begin. Successful partnerships received funding for 10 years with a budget of between £20–60 million each. Lawless et al. (2009) argue that NDC was rooted in two additional assumptions. First, that the unprecedented 10 year time span reflected a belief that deprived areas required longer to 'turn around' than was traditionally allocated by ABIs. Second, that partnerships would address both place based and people based outcomes that is, try to strengthen the culture of the community, whilst also tackling poor levels of educational attainment and employment.

Cochrane argued at the time that perhaps the most important policy development under New Labour was that 'urban regeneration has been reclaimed as a recognisable aspect of social policy' (2000: 191). Indeed, New Labour did identify the importance of urban regeneration in tackling disadvantage and social exclusion (Ginsburg 1999). They argued that letting poor neighbourhoods slide further into the mire was both economically and morally unacceptable and believed that refurbishing communities was integral to tackling the social exclusion of individuals and families by improving the services and opportunities in that area.

In terms of New Labour's formulation of the welfare state, NDC's 'renewal' agenda encompassed both a desire to intervene and alleviate 'unacceptably bad conditions' by supplying additional resources,[1] but also to 'activate the players' (Deacon 2003) by ensuring that partnerships engage with local people to build a sense of ownership and a stake in the renewal of their community (Blears 2003;

---

1   NDC funding was external to mainstream budgets and intended to be spent by communities not local service providers.

Lupton and Power 2005). This synthesis of top-down and bottom-up approaches has been described as an attempt to balance both 'structure and agency in the planning and delivery of social policy' (Alcock 2004: 90). It is also consistent with Giddens' (1998) belief in the importance of refurbishing the physical and social dimensions of community, which should be achieved in partnership with non-state agencies within civil society (Prideaux 2005). For example: 'It has become conventional wisdom that communities need to be involved both in designing what is to be done and in implementing it' (SEU 1998 cited in Dinham 2005: 302). This 'conventional wisdom' was probably also related to an analysis of regeneration policies that failed in the past because they were top-down and paternalistic (Blair 2001). For example, in *Bringing Britain Together*, New Labour stated why it thought previous regeneration policies had failed: 'the absence of effective national policies to deal with the structural causes of decline; a tendency to parachute solutions in from outside, rather than engaging local people' (SEU 1998). At the simplest level, the importance attached to participation of local citizens was premised on policymakers not actually knowing best what communities and individuals require from their public services. Logic followed then that local people should be involved in decision making to mould policies to meet the needs of those at the sharp end of policy delivery. Alcock described this as being about challenging the 'structural tendencies and top-down approaches of past policy planning' (2004: 92). Tony Blair was explicit on this point: 'Too much has been imposed from above, when experience shows that success depends on communities themselves having the power and taking responsibility to make things better' (SEU 1998: 7). This trend towards a 'responsibilising' (Clarke 2005) of 'community' residents as developers and managers of policy, New Labour hoped, would also cement the social infrastructures and sustain vibrant, strong communities over time. That is, New Labour hoped that inclusion in the policymaking process would not only improve the effectiveness of policy (by being more responsive), but would create positive and integrated social networks comprising cohesive, sustainable communities (Lawless et al. 2009). In turn, this would secure the infrastructure of neighbourhoods and in turn generate the 'social capital' (Putnam 2000) necessary to have a 'community safety' effect and ward off anti-social behaviour and criminality (Kearns 2003).

There was, therefore, recognition of the need to try to devise 'bottom up' solutions to local problems that engage residents of regeneration zones. However, it was noted that whilst New Labour may have strengthened the 'turn to community', citizen participation had been called upon to 'reveal or resolve ... the complex problems of urban decline' since the 1970s (Docherty, Goodlad and Paddison 2001: 2226). Alcock traces a longer history arguing that most UK area based programmes have been based on the US 'War on Poverty' campaign of the early 1960s, which was the first to proclaim the importance of the participation of local citizens (2004: 91). However, New Labour were more explicit in emphasising 'partnership', encompassing community consultation and participation in developing proposals for 'renewing' local neighbourhoods (Foley 1999; Imrie and Raco 2003; Rowe and

Devanney 2003). Rouse and Smith (2002) suggest this was part of New Labour's wider democratic renewal agenda that promoted consultation and participation in welfare governance. That is, they wanted to encourage resident participation in the renewal process to foster individual responsibility and a sense of community stakeholding. They hoped this would improve the quality of lives of the poorest and, crucially, sustain vibrant communities once funding streams expired. As Prior has noted: 'the recasting of the citizen as a responsible member of the community ... has been articulated through an emerging governmental discourse of 'civil renewal' (2005: 357). Governance through NDC was concerned with cultivating new forms of identity for local citizens by enabling or expecting them to be active reproducers of ordered 'communities' and custodians of the social wellbeing of the area.

Setting the Scene

A key setting in my analysis of NDC and its impact on residents is the neighbourhood that I visited in the course of this research where I attended resident's meetings, interviewed local people, used services and observed snippets of neighbourhood life. Another setting is the contestation of community within that bounded neighbourhood space structured by various claims, voices and experiences of local residents. My period in the field was, to some degree, a 'search' for community (Brent 2009) in that I sought to understand how this most elusive of ideas, which was designed to be a pivot of the NDC regeneration experience, was understood, mobilised and challenged by residents and other stakeholders in the life of the neighbourhood. This 'search' for community overlapped with attempts to understand how individuals responded to the 'opportunities' afforded by the NDC process and managed their apparent disadvantages as well as an examination of those disadvantages and NDC's attempts to ameliorate them. To set in broader context, it was to explore all of these dynamics within an understanding of NDC as having opened up a new site of governance which drew local residents into a complex nexus of interplaying roles, expectations and demands.

Entering the Field

Upon deciding to conduct some fieldwork in an NDC neighbourhood, I decided there were two intertwined sources of data that were necessary for my investigation – the operation and practice of the NDC programme and the experience of residents relating to their community and to the NDC process. However, before engaging with such decisions and considerations, my first decision was to identify an NDC neighbourhood in which to conduct my fieldwork. My choice of Salford was determined by the proximity of the area to my research base and therefore, accessibility for meetings and interviews. This meant I could also follow any local media coverage of the NDC programme to obtain any additional information through the consumption of local newspapers and television news bulletins. Upon making my decision, I made contact via email with the respective NDC team and after a two-month time gap was invited to meet with the deputy co-ordinator of the New Deal partnership, working there on secondment from the local authority, at the NDC headquarters. Therefore, my entry into the field began, intentionally, in the NDC offices, talking to their staff. The team was made fully aware, indeed, they were keen to know, of my status and background, and were informed explicitly of the intentions of the research. It was decided that the best way to proceed was to make the NDC team aware of my presence and engage with them through interviews with key informants. I hoped that they would then assist me in terms of providing me with NDC literature that would inform me about the structure of NDC, the key individuals involved at the local level, the organisation of meetings and so on. This data would then enable me to build a picture of NDC's reach and operation on the ground, as well as provide useful statistical information about the area that they had collated. They kindly provided me with most key documents although I found out later that one key report (the Participatory Appraisal (PA) team's audit of 'community needs' which was hailed by central government for its innovative consultative techniques and was the key document which 'won' the NDC funding) was not given to me. I was given this later by a resident to illustrate, how, in his eyes NDC's priorities had deviated from those of the community over the initial years of the programme. Nevertheless, having entered the field at the 'official' NDC level, I was then able to navigate my way down to the local level and begin the other dimension of the research and begin interviewing residents. I spent a total of approximately 10 months actually in the field, visiting the NDC area, conducting interviews and attending meetings. Initially, before any contact with local people or NDC staff, regular visits were made to the area during which I walked around the neighbourhood (clearly identifiable from the NDC signage) and used local shops and services. This was undertaken to increase familiarity with the surroundings of the study area and to try to get an untainted impression of it through personal observation (untainted that is by possibly biased local commentary). What I encountered was a small, outer city urban area, constructed around the intersection of a river that runs from east to west and a busy north to south main road. This road snaked rightwards from the main thoroughfare out of Manchester, ran down towards the electoral ward of Charlestown and the basin that encloses the river Irwell before forking through the area of Kersal and disappearing over the hill to the north of the NDC zone. I noticed how this zone was comprised of several distinct housing estates, intermingled with some industrial units and a limited number of shops or public spaces. In the centre of the zone there were large expanses of greenery that extended out from the riverbank. Here, university accommodation could be found surrounded by high security walls, in addition to a grass football pitch and much unused or disused space. The air of dereliction in some parts seemed to betray the reality of a neighbourhood shaped by industrialism and the planning decisions of a different era. It was not hard to see why NDC funding had been allocated here.

As well as the health and wealth inequalities residents of the area experienced, the area appeared rather stagnant and looked like it was struggling to find a post-industrial identity that could revitalise its infrastructure and sense of self. Salford as a whole was undergoing something of a transformation at the time with substantial redevelopment of its canals and docks and it appeared the estates of Charlestown and Lower Kersal (as the NDC zone was called) were to be regenerated in line with the rest of the city. Reading about the zone and surrounding areas, I learned that Salford as a whole had lost almost a third of the city's traditional employment base over the previous 30 years, which was said to have had a marked impact in terms of physical dereliction and social deprivation (Salford Partnership 2002: 7). In 2003, 15 per cent of residents within the NDC zone were not in employment (compared with 9.1 per cent across England), whilst 26.1 per cent were defined as being on a low income (13.3 per cent nationally) (CRESR 2003). According to central government's index of multiple deprivation, Pendleton ward (which contained Charlestown) was ranked 201st (the top 2.4 per cent nationally) and Kersal 1,542nd (top 18.3 per cent) most deprived ward in England (Charlestown and Lower Kersal NDC Partnership 2001a: 5). Salford as a whole, according to Government figures, was the fourth most deprived local authority area in the North West and the 28th nationally (Salford Partnership 2002: 7).

Whilst there may have been some rather sporadic and disjointed pockets of investment and the arrival of university students living in the area, the extent of empty or vandalised housing and lack of facilities in some parts illustrated the reality for most residents. That is, a degree of poverty and neglect combining to produce an area described to me by one resident as 'a forgotten land'. It appeared that NDC had arrived and had set about re-branding the area as a 'community' in an attempt to forge this new identity as a catalyst for investment and regeneration.[2] As we shall see, this new identity would rely substantially on a combination of re-branding and new housing developments following the example of nearby Manchester, which emerged, in the 1990s, from its alleged post-industrial decline as the 'gentrified' renaissance city par excellence.[3] This was in-keeping with a Salford-wide agenda to re-brand certain aspects of the city from sluggish and proletarian to stylish and dynamic and suitable for the young and upwardly mobile. Then-Salford council chief executive John Willis was explicit when he admitted that the archetypal L.S. Lowry image of a 'grimy industrial Salford ... is not the image the council or I want to take into the 21st century.' He added that there was 'huge work to do' to turn Salford into a place where people aspire to live (*Manchester Evening*

---

2   Branding had become a key tool in stimulating economic investment. As Lovering has commented: 'place marketing is now virtually the core activity in local economic development' (1995: 117).

3   This area was not subject to gentrification in the strictest sense in that young, upwardly mobile people and families were to be attracted by *new* build developments, as opposed to inhabiting refurbished inner city properties whether such as apartments,or converted mills and warehouses as became popular in central Manchester.

News 2003: 4). Part of that agenda was to concentrate resources on the nearby Salford Quays dockside development, which was only a short drive away from the NDC zone. This is now a prestige area of vast investment and redevelopment that includes The Lowry hotel and arts centre and the new MediaCity complex which includes the BBC. It is an area of ongoing regeneration around the Manchester Ship Canal and has raised the profile of Salford over the last few years (analogous with the Millennium Dome and London Docklands initiatives). At the time, the contrast with the NDC area and the Pendleton ward in general could not have been more pronounced.

Upon reading about the history of the area, I found that Salford was turned into a key site of industrial production as steam power replaced waterpower during the industrial revolution. It was also at the edge of the Lancashire coalfield, which led to the necessary building of canals and roads then railways. Various industries were built up around the cotton industry and precipitated a population explosion and urban expansion (Frow and Frow 1984: 3). Indeed, Charlestown was one of the earliest working class districts of Victorian Salford, growing around two prominent cotton mills. As the working class of Salford grew, it became an important site for the labour movement as they sought to improve working conditions. Friedrich Engels – an observer of the Salford slums during this time – wrote in 1844:

> If we cross the River Irwell to Salford, we find on a peninsula formed by the river a town of eighty thousand inhabitants, which properly speaking is one large working men's quarter … Hence it is that an old and therefore very unwholesome, dirty and ruinous locality is to be found here … All Salford is built in courts or narrow lanes, so narrow, that they remind me of the narrowest I have ever seen, the little lanes of Genoa … if anyone takes the trouble to pass through these lanes, and glance through the open doors and windows into the houses and cellars, he can convince himself afresh with every step that the workers of Salford live in dwellings in which cleanliness and comfort are impossible (1969: 95).

It was these conditions that the labour movement sought to improve through both political and radical means. There were large, influential branches of Owenite reformism and the Chartist movement (which organised the famous demonstration on Kersal Moor in 1839) in Salford, as well as vibrant trade union activity. Into the twentieth century, the Labour party began to win local seats in Salford elections. In 1935, they gained control of the city council – which they have retained ever since, apart from a blip in 1967–69 when the Conservatives seized control (Frow and Frow 1984: 24). Currently, Labour dominates Salford city council with 36 councillors alongside 13 Conservatives and 13 Liberal Democrats. At the 2008 local elections three of the four wards that extend into the NDC zone returned Labour majorities and one Liberal Democrat victory. Turnout was approximately 26 per cent across these wards compared with 31 per cent across the city (http://www.salford.gov.uk/council/elections.htm).

Since the loss of its traditional industries (the foundations of one cotton mill in Charlestown are still visible today), Salford has been subject to a range of urban programmes and regeneration initiatives. Surrounding the central Quays redevelopment, there have been four Single Regeneration Budget schemes, two of which bordered the NDC area. As well as New Deal for Communities funding, Salford secured three spending rounds of Sure Start and over £100 million in European Union and National Lottery funding. Parts of the city have also received money from the Housing Market Renewal Fund and were classed as part of Health Action Zones (Salford Partnership 2002: 95).

Negotiating Community and Generating Data

The NDC model of community contained assumptions about what residents are and should be like in terms of relationships, actions, needs, experiences – predicated on an eliding of the spatial and social. My research goal was to generate data that sought to reflect upon the propriety and effectiveness of this model by exploring dimensions of community which challenge it – processes of conflict and contestation within the community. This objective was partly driven by a reaction to traditional 'community studies' which provided romanticised, partial accounts of community life imbued with 'theoretical and ideological bias' (Fremeaux 2005: 268). My study was a conscious attempt to unearth some of the complexities and tensions in local life to provide a counterbalance to the overly positive descriptions inherent in past accounts and a tentative attempt to question policy interventions based on these nostalgic assumptions. Ontologically, these themes stem from a foregrounding of how social agents experience and negotiate their environment (and thereby, interact) as the critical factors in the (dis)functioning of community. This is also a stance that views meaning and interpretation by social agents as partially constitutive of social reality and of community itself. Epistemologically, this implies that useful knowledge lies primarily in the relationships within and between those social agents who I contend are active in *doing* community. Methodologically, there were two levels at which knowledge about 'conflict' between residents could be generated. One was at an observable, superficial level where data might be produced 'externally', that is, by an individual not involved in the dispute, but commenting upon it. An example from my dataset would be: 'My neighbours are always at each others throats' (male resident, under 21). Clearly, this tells me nothing about the nature of the conflict because the person relaying it to me was an observer rather than a participant. Nevertheless, it is a useful piece of data that provides me with some 'evidence' albeit rather limited and in need of elaboration, of conflict within the study area. This kind of 'evidence' was also found in local NDC-commissioned reports which mentioned some form of conflict expressed to NDC (such as between local youths and older people). This provided me with some pertinent 'issues' that I could explore further in my interviews with young and older people, as well as a basic indication that these conflicts existed. The other level concerned data that participants in particular disputes actually generated. This data is more likely to be contextual and offer insights into motivations and meanings on the part of the respondents, although obviously this depends, to an extent, on skilled interviewing and a sympathetic interviewee. So, for example, when a respondent remarked: 'I'd like to take the rubbish and dump it back into their [gypsies] site' (female resident, over 60, brackets added), she was identifying a source of conflict about which she had strong views and it was my responsibility as researcher to probe further about this issue and generate useful data about it. This level is possibly more fruitful because it provides access to the values and norms that motivate conflict, which has more interesting explanatory potential in terms of exploring how and why communities are contested.

Agency

NDC's model of agency promotes what residents are and should be like in terms of behaviour and actions towards other residents, their community and the NDC process. Again, my intention was to generate data that reflected upon the appropriateness and effectiveness of this model by exploring dimensions of individual agency that challenged that model –the extent of community feeling and 'neighbourliness' as well as disinterest and apathy amongst residents. Ontologically, this agenda accepted the view of social reality as constituted by individual agents all 'doing' community in different and often conflicting ways. Such a position renders any attempt, through policy mechanisms, to 'promote' certain forms of behaviour or community as suspicious because it is failing to conceptualise that 'reality' suitably and is neglecting the different forms of experience that constitute it. Epistemologically, this again privileges individual accounts and emphasises the importance of understanding how agents negotiate their 'field'. However, like community, data can also be generated from observations made by outsiders, or from quantitative data (statistics that indicate community involvement in NDC business for example). Again, where the research revolves around an exploration of themes or concepts, then different methodological approaches can be utilised to generate relevant data.

Exclusion

NDC's model was predicated on the ways New Labour constructs residents as excluded – in terms of their needs, experiences and capabilities. To examine the value of such a model I tried to generate data that explored the various ways social exclusion is experienced within the same geographical space, as well as examining relationships between residents as processes that can shape the way exclusion is experienced. Ontologically, this infers that social exclusion is a condition not only determined by an absence of material goods such as money or decent housing, but also shaped by social relations. That is, that the structural conditions of 'exclusion' are actively *lived* by agents through interaction with others, which can ease or exacerbate the conditions in which they find themselves. Again, in terms of epistemology, it follows that valid 'knowers' are residents themselves and a suitable research method must strive to interpret the experiences of local residents and their interactions.

Conclusion

The purpose of this chapter has been to do a little more unpacking of NDC introduce the background to my fieldwork in order to prepare the ground for subsequent discussions. It should be clear by now that my goal is to offer a critical perspective of the models of social relations that NDC embodies. I contend that these can be traced back to a particular agenda of New Labour that sought to reframe welfare and rearticulate the meaning of individual citizenship, all within an increasing trend towards layered governance. The next three chapters unpack the three key models of NDC in more detail and combine critical insights from the literature and the fieldwork introduced in this chapter to evaluate the NDC experience for residents. This is by way of laying the foundations for a final rounded discussion about the impact of NDC on the autonomy and political status of resident citizens.

Chapter 4

Contesting Community

Introduction

It has been considered important in this discussion to offer some context to the NDC programme; to situate and locate it within a broader milieu of social welfare and attempted reforms in order to provide a sense of both intellectual and political context. The goal of this chapter is to start to unpack NDC in more detail and focus on the three key concepts – community, agency and exclusion – which, as I saw it, distilled, framed and drove the practice of the programme as a mechanism for achieving social change in selected poor neighbourhoods. This had important implications for the individuals who inhabited the NDC space and I consider how the interpretation and implementation of each of these concepts represented a problematic aspect of the NDC experience. Starting with community, the next three chapters will argue how these concepts constituted facets of the NDC process before drawing on literature and data from the fieldwork described in Chapter 3 to problematise each in turn. I synthesise and apply relevant data in order to critically assess these concepts, which represent the analyses, frameworks and objectives that underpin New Labour's attempt to regenerate civic space and individual behaviour as a means of rearticulating citizenship and addressing social exclusion. My critiques of what we might term the contingencies of the regeneration process are elucidated in such a manner to engage constructively with theories of community, agency and exclusion. I do not claim or attempt to have unearthed definitive understandings of each but do try to feel my way towards more nuanced accounts. In this regard, my analysis operates with and beyond NDC and New Labour and before returning to the implications of my analysis in Chapter 7, these next three chapters offer not only critique, but a constructive, sociological engagement with some difficult terrain.

NDC and the 'Recognisable' Community?

As explored in Chapter 2, New Labour's enthusiasm for 'community' has been well documented and its Communitarian progenitors consistently evoked (for example, Driver and Martell 1997; Levitas 2000; Heron 2001; Deacon 2002; Imrie and Raco 2003; Prideaux 2005). There was an aspiration to 'build', 'strengthen' and 'empower' 'active communities' (Blair 1998; Blears 2003) that reflected a normative, quasi – moral belief in community as a mechanism which could nurture responsible citizenship. It was through community that citizens would uphold their civic duties through paid employment, volunteering and social entrepreneurship. NDC was an expression of a dual belief in both the existence of communities as stable entities inhabited by people and families with similar needs and values; as well as the positive benefits of promoting community as a moral framework to engender civic renewal, maintain social order and ameliorate social exclusion. The construction of community as a unified entity was inscribed in NDC planning and implementation decisions. A great deal of focus was placed on 'choosing the right neighbourhood' that would have 'the greatest capacity to turn themselves around' in initial government guidelines for prospective partnerships. Furthermore, guidelines stated that NDC areas should be 'recognisable communities (less than 4,000 households) with a strong sense of identity and shared aspirations' (NRU 2001: 8). Through an elision of spatial and social forms, each NDC neighbourhood was chosen in part because it was perceived to meet these criteria, showing that a spatially determined community sense had to pre-exist government spending via NDC. New Labour appeared to want to reward what it considered 'correct' expressions of community and calculated that it could harness these dispositions in order to get a positive financial and social return on its investment. In so doing, they imbued selected spatial entities with socio-civic properties generated by the assumed identity and historicity possessed by these places. What this meant for those areas of material disadvantage that were 'unrecognisable' communities is a moot point. Nevertheless, the privileging of areas 'suitable' for NDC funding illustrates that New Labour viewed these areas as unitary, stable spaces where local residents had a shared and consistent flow of experience of exclusion and community that NDC could harness. This is how they believed NDC could work – that residents had sufficient shared interest to need and want to row in the same direction and essentially renew themselves and their social and civic spaces. By implication, this relegated those areas deemed to lack unity and accord as being unable or unwilling to construct a viable, self-fulfilling community and therefore benefit from civic welfare support in the form of NDC. Nonetheless, in my case study area, the importance of possessing community in gaining access to NDC resources was recognised by Salford NDC Partnership who emphasised the 'strong sense of community' present in the area, where people are 'there for each other' whilst stressing the importance of not letting 'the good people mov(e) out' (Charlestown and Lower Kersal NDC Partnership 2001a). To some degree, this reflects the internalising of policy logics by local decision makers and planners who were complicit in the construction of local spaces as coherent, investable entities. In responding to these logics in order to secure funding, they buttressed and entrenched the model of community which framed their practice. However, this is not simply a matter of local acquiescence to central demands, since it also points to a complex interplay between local and central government, highlighted in Chapter 3, where the form and substance of New Labour's governance 'invitation' to citizens and sub-national spaces was predicated on an attempted empathetic understanding of the local-social. That is, the model of community at play through NDC was one that was infused, in part, with an analysis of what 'responsible' 'active' local citizens want and need. Consequently, we can observe a discourse of community, fertilised at central and at local policymaking level, with assumptive understandings of what community 'is' and what 'it' needs, enacted by and through the NDC process. This is policy as a discursive product of the community it seeks to assist.

Of course, this process operated within the NDC neighbourhoods themselves, in which the physical and social space of each place was drawn into the (re)enactment of community. In Salford, NDC was an explicit presence in the regeneration zone. Its office was located in the centre of the zone and the NDC slogan was attached to everything from street cleaning vehicles to school gates in an attempt to brand the space explicitly as an 'NDC community'. Furthermore, it was active in galvanising resident participation, manifesting in an expectation that residents should coalesce around and help 'create' the community. It did this by encouraging residents to conceptualise their immediate locale as 'their' community, by consulting them about improvements and problems of that bounded place and through an array of signifiers such as meetings, newsletters and the physical erection of signs that delineated and reified it as a community space. This process of 'image management' (Dean and Hastings 2000) is not just an important component of regeneration practice on the ground, but it reflects how the construction and maintenance of a particular community discourse was constituted at every stage in the implementation of NDC and valorised through models of responsible local citizenship consisting of an identification with and emotional commitment to local place. Community became a socio-spatial product with parameters, norms and boundaries in which residents were entangled. Why this was problematic and how this process was challenged by residents are key themes of this discussion.

An important feature of the production of community was its relationship with individual behaviour and morality. At a central policy level, Government Ministers reified community consistently in their language of individual responsibility being linked to the communal and the importance of accountability to the collective (Flint and Nixon 2006: 941). This often tended to manifest in discussions of 'punishments' for 'yob' and antisocial behaviour through public name and shame campaigns and increased input for residents in the reporting and deciding of punishment of minor offences in their communities (for example, see http://www.direct.gov.uk/en/CrimeJusticeAndTheLaw/PrisonAndProbation/ DG_182080). The idea being that by locating individual behaviour within a community context, moral and behavioural reconstruction could occur, either as an incentive to be part of the community, or by legitimising punishments with reference to 'communal' values being transgressed. Above all, there was a presupposition of a minority of residents who need community, alongside those 'responsible' citizens who represent the community. This reflected a belief in a behavioural fault line within excluded spaces between the consensual majority and a deviant minority of unruly residents that cause social disorder and require a moralising voice. New Labour's communities, therefore, had behavioural and moral parameters that determined entry and membership and were deployed as mechanisms to both reconstruct citizenship and police, moralise and reconstruct 'suspect' behaviour. Programmes like NDC were designed to be repositories for the operationalising of the 'responsible' voice and provide a mechanism by which the responsible feel 'empowered' and the 'bad' behaviour of the transgressors be locally reconstructed.

This construction of community was not just viewed as an instrument of moral regeneration, but also as a means for protecting excluded residents. It appears the reification of excluded spaces as communities (alongside increased opportunities in education and welfare to work strategies) containing strong local networks, or 'social capital', was viewed as providing a bulwark against the dislocating and fragmentary forces of social exclusion. Therefore, it was a legitimate goal of policy to assist or construct strong local relationships:

> An influential perspective on these matters is that neighbourhood decline sets in train a cumulative decline in social capital. Networks are disrupted and weakened, population turnover erodes familiarity and trust, and policies and initiatives aimed at reversing the decline are being implemented in a context of community disengagement and disillusionment (Forrest and Kearns 2001: 21–39).

Increasingly, communities are codified as spaces that 'deserve' security in order that residents can enjoy them. As Flint and Nixon have noted, definitions of civility and ethical conduct have expanded from individualist obligations to those based on a shared sense of space and respect for the community. Therefore, residents are expected to behave appropriately, keep gardens and homes in good order and, ultimately challenge the behaviour of others (2006: 950). Again, the idea of these expectations as being integral 'to' community had a basis in New Labour's attempt to offer citizens a model for civic life that they thought people wanted. It is no revelation that key politicians such as Blair, Blunkett and Blears as well as policymakers such as Louise Casey – former head of the 'Respect Task Force' – sought to identify and articulate the needs of a particular section of the 'respectable' working and middle classes whom they saw as electorally important and socially intrinsic. This 'decent' majority were considered in need of defending and rewarding and part of that process was to deploy criminal and civil justice rhetoric to assuage the fears and contentions of these groups. This stratified model nuances our understanding of New Labour and community as it demonstrates that there was, ostensibly, some account of social division. Again, NDC was an enactment of a particular model of the local-social and was designed to purposely strengthen the respectable voice as the division between 'decent' and deviant became more easily operational in order to discipline the minority of problematic residents whilst defining and shaping the socio-spatial product of community.

De-stabilising Community

Whilst New Labour believed in the existence and positive effect of belonging to a community – a social relation deriving from spatial proximity and shared material conditions, there is a strong body of literature that has questioned the meaning of community as a coherent spatially-determined entity. Firstly, many observers have questioned the notion of unified spatial communities, pointing out that division is actually an integral component: 'Community is as much about struggle as it is about unity' (Brent 1997: 83). Brent argues that such entities are often defined in response to an excluded 'other' and cites examples of how the creation of 'insider' and 'outsider' groupings is part of 'community construction' (1997: 82). Similarly, Crow and Allan have identified the need to recognise, 'the social construction of communities and the negotiated nature of their terms of membership'. They continue by arguing that, 'precisely what it takes to be accepted as 'one of us' varies enormously from place to place and also between different types of social groups' (1994: xvii). Day and Murdoch noted insider/outsider divisions in their study of a community in rural Wales. They illustrated the realities of being an incomer to a community, and the difficulties 'new' people or families can face (1993: 103). Similarly, Payne cites the 'key issue' creating conflict in his study of a rural village is 'between locals and incomers' (1992: 19). He describes how being 'born and bred' is a flexible 'rule' mobilised to exclude 'those whom locals wish to define as outsiders' (1992: 19). Social closure of this kind is a recurring theme in the community studies literature. For example, Frankenberg notes that, 'In all the studies there is a history of conflict between the new and the old which goes far to determine the social patterns of the new. The old inhabitants did not choose to have a council estate and indeed often fought bitterly against its being built' (1965: 199). Warwick and Littlejohn, in their study of coalmining areas found:

> The labour force which was assembled was drawn from a wide range of localities, and the sense of mobility which marked this assembly was sufficient to raise some doubts about how far this could or would become the basis of relatively homogeneous and solidary "working class communities". Many internal conflicts based in rivalry between 'locals' and 'incomers ... The longer you live in a locality, the more likely it is that you become integrated, but you can still carry the stigma of being a "foreigner". There are still jokes in Ashby about "Staffies", that is migrants from Staffordshire ... that were meant to raise a laugh about outsiders who were rather slow in "learning the ropes" or were deviant in some way (1992: 82).

This trend towards 'social closure' illustrates how community can be a constructed and negotiated entity which pivots around questions of access and belonging, often shaped by dynamics of power deriving from length of residence, housing tenure, gender, age, ethnicity and a variety of other social divisions. According to Elias and Scotson, community is the product of the 'universal regularity of any established-outsider figuration' (1994: xvi). Furthermore, Neuwirth suggests: 'Certain groups of a community may affect closure which is directed against other community subgroups. Communities are not necessarily socially or economically homogeneous, but may develop their own internal stratification systems' (cited in Warwick and Littlejohn 1992: 13). In Salford, I spoke to one resident who was directly involved in policing what he considered to be the integrity and safety of the community:

> What we do with smack dealers is we kick 'em out. We don't wait for the council or the police to do it. We go down ... throw all the furniture on the streets and they've got to go, 'cos they can't live there ... If they don't listen then, we fucking drag 'em out ... We've done it 5 or 6 times over the last 4 or 5 years. The reason why we haven't got a smack problem round here is because we don't let it happen ... once they start selling to young kids and once you get 1 or 2 young kids on it, you get 5 or 6 on it. Well, we're not having it, so we don't have it and it's our direct action ('Jim', resident; 21–60).

This is a rather extreme example, but it illustrates how definitions of suitability and belonging can infuse community. It is clearly problematic to attempt to 'read off' unity of values and positive social bonds from a spatial grouping. Communities are politicised social spaces in which groups and individuals stake claims and ascribe divergent rules and codes, bringing into play wider dynamics of power and social division. The key challenge offered here therefore is that a more nuanced account of community is one which does not deny its possibilities or existence per se, since as Brent (2009) points out and some of the examples of social closure indicate, it would be fatuous to entirely deny or obscure the spatial component of community when mobilised as a resource by activist citizens defending place or culture. Rather, it is one which seeks to challenge the spatial determinism of so much community thinking and analysis and tries to conceive of community as a complex space subject to divisions, tensions and ruptures. This is a necessary challenge if we consider the rich tradition of community studies that tends to neglect the uncomfortable or complex realities of their research communities. Crow and Allan identified these romanticised accounts as conveying, 'only solidarity and co-operation...ignoring the schism and conflict in local social life, highlighting the positive, celebrated sides of communities and neglecting their oppressive and coercive aspects' (1994: 2). Similarly, Fremeaux has asserted: 'the ideological stance taken on community led these traditional studies to offer an interpretation of relationships characterised by harmony, affection, consensus and stability, whilst overlooking the coercion and power relations that occur both externally and internally' (2005: 268). Moreover, Crow and Allan argue that the community studies tradition was guilty of neglecting 'issues relating to gender inequalities', using 'malestream language' and focusing 'on the public sphere' (1994: 16). For Cain and Yuval Davis, these accounts reflected some particular cultural assumptions: 'Social policy conceptions of 'the community' have often ignored marginal sections in the population. The intimate, close and rooted image of 'the community' implied a homogeneity composing family, neighbourhood and parish, all of whom conformed to a hegemonic culture, often English and usually working class' (cited in Pereira 1997: 15). Bell and Newby have been similarly critical and, quoting Ruth Glass, denounce community studies as, 'the poor sociologist's substitute for the novel' (1971: 13), due to their perceived preference for cosy description rather than sociological insight. Geoff Payne has contributed to the critique of community studies stating that the working class were portrayed as 'heroic' – 'hard working, hard drinking, independent minded, but mutually supportive' and that the 'downside' of community: 'poverty, patriarchy, excessive social control and intolerance of individuality' was overlooked by researchers (Payne 1992: 17). Robert Roberts, in his personal account of the 'classic slum' in Salford identifies a similar trend: 'some sociologists have been apt to write fondly about the cosy gregariousness of the old slum dwellers. Their picture, I think, has been overdrawn. Close propinquity, together with cultural poverty, led as much to enmity as it did to friendship. There could be much unhappiness and fear of one neighbour by another ...' (cited in Bell and Newby 1971: 30). Roberts also asserts his belief that the slum had its own distinctive class structure ranging from elite 'leading families' – 'shopkeepers, publicans, skilled tradesmen' (1971: 5) – down to a social base of the 'lowest of the low' – 'bookies runners, idlers, part-time beggars and petty thieves' (1971: 8) manifesting in pervasive intra-class social divisions.

Part of this lack of analysis may have been down to methodological errors on the part of research teams. For example, Cornwell's 1984 study of health and illness in Bethnal Green observed that there is often a contradiction between respondents' public and private accounts of community life:

> Uncritical acceptance of people's public accounts as literal truths leads inevitably to romanticism of the past ... Private accounts ... reveal a darker side, including the "turning of the blind eye" to other people's troubles; as well as the open doors and the familiarity with others, it included the arguments, fights and brawls, particularly over children, and the petty snobberies that kept people apart from each other (cited in Crow and Allan 1994: 20).

Furthermore, the impulse to mythologise spatially-bounded communities may come from assumptions about proletarian bonhomie in the face of hardship – a key narrative in much defensive left wing political rhetoric and unthinking traditional social policy which feared analysing too closely the realities of poor neighbourhoods in case of accusations of victim blaming. These images and myths of the spirited, close-knit working class have been represented and reproduced through popular television and film as well as the social research cited here. Nonetheless, we should not be deceived by the sentimental, 'gemeinshaft' (Tönnies 1967) visions of community that permeated such texts, although they do provide an insight into the construction of community as a positive and romantic ideal and how academic researchers have been complicit in creating such mythology. They also help us understand why successive governments have 'fallen' for community given the 'warm associations' it evokes (Herbert 2005) and the cohesive properties with which it is imbued.

However, despite the shortcomings of the community studies canon, there are also numerous examples of research which seeks to offer a more nuanced analysis of how communities (dis)function. This body of research – much of it conducted by feminist scholars – expresses how such accounts of a 'public' community life give inadequate space to experiences shaped by gender, ethnicity, disability and other social divisions, which can reveal the sometimes-uncomfortable 'private' truths of living in certain areas. This opens up the possibility of analysing community as a social space negotiated by residents and mediated by social division. Spatiality is a factor, but only one amid many constituents of community. For example, Fiona Williams identified how the threat of racial abuse or violence can lead black men and women to feel uncomfortable within, ostensibly, their own community. She points out how a combination of racism and sexism, poverty and local housing resources and policies, can imprison black women in their neighbourhoods in very specific ways and cites a quotation from Bryan et al. (1985):

> The accumulated effects of twenty-five years of racist housing policies have ensured that growing numbers of black women are imprisoned on the upper floors of dilapidated tower blocks in every inner-city with little hope of escape. If our white neighbours harass us, or if our men abuse us, we often have no choice but to leave, exposing ourselves and our children to the traumas of homelessness (cited in Williams 1997: 38).

This is a theme emphasised by Worley (2005) who argues that the use of the term community by policymakers obscures the racialised and often gendered way in which communities are reproduced. Crow and Allan noted:

> Given the importance of social divisions that are maintained within these communities, in what sense is it sensible to talk of a single community? ... What these issues force us to realise is the inappropriateness of conceptualising communities in terms of firm boundaries, fixed membership and rigid patterns of inclusion and exclusion (1994: 189).

Hoggett (1997) has stated,

> ... each neighbourhood is a site for a multitude of networks, interests and identities ... what comes across, even from the strongly working class neighbourhoods, is the heterogeneity and complexity of communities. And yet it is this that policymakers and practitioners still seem to be largely unaware of (1997: 15).[1]

---

1   See also Ginsburg (1999) and Foley and Martin (2000) for similar sentiments about heterogeneous 'communities'.

We can see therefore how New Labour's apparent belief that certain spatial configurations would translate into a sense of kinship with shared norms and values amongst its members deserves to be problematised. This could be particularly pertinent if, as Bauman argues, poverty and 'community' are considered incommensurate:

> Ghetto life does not sediment community. Sharing stigma and public humiliation does not make the sufferers into brothers; it feeds mutual derision, contempt and hatred ... ghetto experience dissolves solidarity and destroys mutual trust before they have been given a chance to take roots. A ghetto is not a greenhouse of community feelings. It is on the contrary a laboratory of social disintegration, atomization and anomie ... To sum up: ghetto means the impossibility of community' (2001: 122).

Brent (1997) expresses this debate succinctly when he notes that: 'Communities are not oases of equality where major issues of power magically stop at the boundary' (1997: 80). Researchers have found social divisions rooted in class, employment, gender, age, ethnic differences that make and remake community and often determine the allocation of resources and power within defined spaces. Such divisions play an important part in the quality of life experienced by residents and can prevent certain groups from using local services (e.g David Page's (2002) study of Thames Green). Similarly, Linda East in her study of an estate in Nottingham found that: 'Divisions based on age, gender, class and ethnicity proved to be more important in shaping the lives of local residents than shared geographical space. This brings into question the concept of community-level social capital where 'community' is interpreted to mean the people sharing a particular locality' (2002: 170). Her research revealed the heterogeneity of needs within an excluded space (defined in this case according to government deprivation indices) and the variety of experiences of users of services funded by regeneration programmes. In a similar vein, Coffield has noted that community life was characterised by a number of divisions, some of which were peculiar to the 1980s, others which had deep-seated antecedents: '[divisions] between those who supported the (1984–5 miners') strike and those who did not ... between the employed and the jobless; between those who 'shop' their neighbours to the DHSS and those who do not ... between those who can afford to buy their council houses and those who cannot (Coffield 1986, cited in Crow and Allan 1994: 54). Bea Campbell, in her study of communities across the UK experiencing rioting and civil unrest, uncovered the heterogeneity of such places and the range of divisions that exist despite apparent consensus:

> What was new in the Eighties and Nineties was that riot became routine. Its persistent resurgence demands that we ask new questions about community, solidarity, law and disorder among men and women living with desperate local economies. Fissured by gender and generation, race and class, the riots of the

Nineties are as much against community as they are about it; indeed, they render
the very concept of "community" problematic (1993: xi).

Campbell sought to reveal some of the internal dynamics of local 'communities'
and more often than not, it was young men who were viewed as destructive agents
that undermined the fabric of the public sphere:

> Cedarwood's Wellbeing women's group bought exercise equipment – a treadmill,
> a rower and a bike – and kept it in the building's secure room. Once when it
> was empty a hole was hammered through the wall. Everything went: exercise
> equipment, typewriters, kettles, photocopier ... it was also in the conquest of
> space, other people's space, that these boys were constituting themselves as men
> ... What they admired was the criminalised brotherhood; what they harassed
> and hurt was community politics. It was an entirely and explicitly gendered
> formation. A voluble woman active in the Credit Union went into the youth
> project, a reincarnation of the old Book Centre, and was greeted by a cold
> chorus: "Fucking whoring cunt ... fucking twat ...". She never went there again
> (1993: 244).

Community in such areas then becomes a space in which identities are negotiated,
forged and asserted. For Campbell, young men did this by attacking other
community members. Crucially, it was a 'gendered formation' – an assertion
of dominance or defiance that mobilised entrenched social divisions, a process
that occurred despite the alleged unity of poor or excluded spaces. Amin (2002)
in his analysis of the 2001 disturbances in Oldham and elsewhere has discussed
a similar dynamic between white and non-white ethnic groups who have: 'a
strong sense of place ... but one based on turf claims, or when shared, defended
in exclusionary ways ... spaces (that) in reality support multiple publics' (2002:
972). Therefore, rather than containing a 'unitary sense of place', communities
should be viewed as spaces in which identities and needs are negotiated, often
producing divisions and contestations as well as solidarity amongst residents.
It is these sorts of dimensions of community that leads some to ask the crucial
question: 'who is it that has the power to define and represent "community", and
at whose expense' (Day 1996: 152).

Contesting Community

Taking on board the literature which draws attention to the ruptures and
complexities that are part of the negotiation and struggle of community, I set out
to generate data in the field in Salford that would examine and explore how the
residents of this particular neighbourhood deployed, challenged and experienced
the kinds of relationships and behaviours that are considered to comprise a cohesive
community. The concept of contestation was central to this in that it informed all

other discussions about conflict and division. Several authors have emphasised the contested and diverse nature of spatially bounded communities (e.g. Brent 1997; Foley and Martin 2000; Dinham 2005) and some have examined the implications for developing local networks of support and trust in heterogeneous localities (e.g. Taylor 2000a). The first point to make is that contestation is a relational process because it involves examples of the comparison of two or more sets of values or perspectives. Additionally, it could be an example of overt contestation, not just of viewpoints, but either everyday conflict between people or groups, or space, whereby groups of residents clash over the use of some communal area, facility or territory. Therefore, there are two separate spheres of knowledge that can be used as data: that which relates to contrasting values (relating to needs, both of individuals and of the neighbourhood as a whole, about NDC, or about other social groups) and data documenting explicit conflicts between residents. One community representative thought the needs of the area as a whole were self-evident: 'I think there are so many different aspirations because there are so many different issues to aspire to, or about. But, in general terms, I think there is an awful lot of consensus about the problems of the area. Because they are the problems of the area, and they can see them!' ('Bill', resident and community representative: 21–60). One of the tasks when interviewing, highlighted by this quote, was to ensure respondents did not talk just about a vague notion of the 'needs of the area' as this tended to be around environmental things like cleaning streets or generalised comments about poor shopping amenities. What made such data meaningful was if it was related to their own personal experience. For example, older male residents spoke of a poor bus service in their part of the NDC zone. An issue exacerbated by their age, inability to drive and the cost of alternatives, such as taxis. This gave a more productive insight into how the lack of a facility affected certain groups and what other factors contributed to their needs.

This exploration of community and the extent of its contestation is split into three parts. Firstly, the use of two examples of conflicting needs will illustrate how individuals and groups living in the same place do not necessarily share the same perspective and that the contestation is rooted in different social locations within that space. Secondly, another example is used to illustrate that contestation is not just about needs or physical space, but also around an idea of territory and associated constructions of 'deservingness' and 'belonging'. Finally, data is explored that illustrates how contestations of physical space add another dimension to the destabilising of community

Local Conflicting Needs: Policing

The first example came from discussions of policing in the NDC area. Each resident interviewed was asked about their feelings on the policing of the NDC zone and about 'community safety and security' generally. Perhaps unsurprisingly, the young people interviewed were almost unanimous in their verdict: 'enough of them round 'ere' (male resident: under 21), 'community safety and security? What the fuck do we want that for? Got loads of them (police) round here' (male resident: under 21) and 'all the po po do is moan, 'nough of them round here' (female resident: under 21).

There was no appetite for a stronger policing presence, although some did recognise the importance of community security generally. This was in contrast to the perception of older residents that police were ineffectual, if not invisible: 'Police? Who are they, aliens?' (male resident: over 60). The group of older men particularly wanted greater police visibility to prevent youths riding on motorbikes 'terrorising the neighbourhood' – an example, not just of conflicting perceptions of policing, but also how a broader struggle over the use of space, values and behaviour inevitably shapes the sense of priorities for the police and other agencies. These kinds of struggles tended not to be realised day to day because young and old, for example, experience little interaction, but manifested in contestations of space or in conflicts over how to protect that space, such as policing. One older female echoed the sentiment of a lack of police presence in the area when she recounted this story: 'I saw a policeman once and asked, 'can I ask you a question. Are you a mirage?" This generational difference in perception was confirmed by the NDC sector sergeant: 'Yeah, because the elderly want to see high profile police for obviously the security feeling. The youths want us to get off their backs. They are, erm, always on the streets and we're always moving them on because of all the complaints.'

Whereas young people felt that they were over-policed, many residents experienced a degree of vulnerability, especially in the evening, which created a desire for increased security through more CCTV cameras, curfews on young people or a more visible police presence. Curfews, suggested in the Participatory Appraisal (PA)[2] team report, presumably in response to similar feelings expressed by older people, were a controversial topic for some young people. Two of my respondents identified their impracticality, one arguing that his mother wanted him out of the house 'when she comes in from work', or after dinner. One young male made the point that curfews would: '... cause chaos – everyone would break them and the police would be round arresting everybody and putting them in jail' (Male resident: under 21). One adult respondent – a youth worker, was against the idea, arguing that young people were blamed for many of the problems in the area and that curfews were not only unworkable, but were an ineffectual response to the issue of youths out after dark:

---

2 Participatory appraisal is a community research technique pioneered in the international development field. This NDC was introduced to it through a local Oxfam connection. Through this method local people can express their views and be directly involved in planning projects and defining policy goals. It involves using basic tools such as flip charts and so on and its emphasis is on going to the community for ideas, rather than expecting people to come forward and participate (Charlestown and Lower Kersal Delivery Plan 2001: 10).

Young people should be taught responsibility and enabled to improve their own lives, not punished, especially when marginalised … a breach of human rights really. If you said black people or gay people are not allowed out after 9pm then there would be an outcry, but because they are young it seems to be okay ('Paul', youth worker: 21–60).

The suggestions to the PA team for curfews, a 'three strikes and you are out' policy and so on illustrates how it is the 'problem' of young people that is part of this desire for more or better policing. This is not a difference of opinion per se, but part of a deeper question about the relationship of young people to the rest of their community and the behavioural expectations being placed upon them. This echoes what Lee has suggested regarding children being constructed as 'out of place' if they are on the streets and outside adult supervision. He notes how they are blamed for social problems and treated as 'a well-spring of social disorder' (2001: 69). It also reflects the work done by Phillips and Smith on incivility and how young people's occupation of public space tends to mean they are assumed to be the worst perpetrators requiring the most surveillance (2003: 105). This is in contrast to their findings that illustrate how incivility is common across all ages – including those considered 'respectable' citizens (2003: 104).

To add complexity to this division, the student respondents, despite being young people, were in favour of increased police presence because of their perceived vulnerability as 'outsiders' in a 'rough' area:

C: Probably impossible to police areas like this what are full of scallies. It's known as a rough area so. They could probably do more … Seems strange but the only time I see police walking round Salford is always in the middle of the afternoon.

J: During the day yeah.

C: Where if they said if any police walking round on the beat had to go to about say eight nine o'clock on a night … If they were gonna walk about around ten o'clock, eleven o'clock when yobs start, well it's not yobs, it's young kids, if they were walking about at them times, or even if young kids thought there was a heavier police presence then there'd maybe not be antisocial behaviour.

J: I think it goes on later than 10 o'clock into the middle of the night. If you've got to get somewhere – to uni or the computer room, or if you are just coming home from a night out you know you are completely unprotected you haven't anyone who is around who can try and stop anything. There is no police, no cameras to pick up anything to inform other people. You've just got no security whatsoever unless you're on the phone.

Another young male who was resident at a local hostel for homeless young people conveyed an appetite for increased security for the hostel – more security and cameras to protect from other local young males who have attacked the centre in the past. However, this was tempered by a rejection of more police ('don't want more of them round here!'). Another interesting difference around policing came from within the refugee community in the NDC zone. The local asylum seeker support worker described to me how some African refugees were very wary of the police, whilst refugees from other areas viewed them as essential to their sense of security.

We can see therefore, that depending upon the social location of the groups or individuals concerned within the neighbourhood, there were differing attitudes to the policing of the area. However, most (including students) seemed united in their perception of a need for protection from local 'scallies' or deviant young people. It was apparent from speaking to those young people that they felt the effects of that perception.

Housing Redevelopment

Another conflicting need related to the physical redevelopment plans for the NDC zone which came to be the key strategy in the regeneration of this area. The plans included a programme of demolition of council housing stock, renovation of other housing and plans for building private apartments on the riverside. At the time that they were first mooted, these plans created a lot of resistance from some residents, particularly those affected by demolition. A poster campaign was launched and made visible around the affected estates once residents were aware of the plans. Slogans on posters and graffiti such as 'Not another urban snatch', 'Renovation not relocation' and 'No to New Deal' came to dominate some parts of the NDC zone. The local authority removed the posters from the main roadsides, but according to one resident, were too afraid to remove those inside the estates. This programme of resistance was successful in reversing demolition plans for some streets through the organisation of petitions and surveys of local opinion:

> What happened up here, they wanted to knock down 30-odd old pit houses most of them privately owned, but they were having none of it this community and they turned round and said, "fuck off" you're not having any of it. They (NDC) did the same surveys we did and our last survey came back "we don't wanna go", so they couldn't get them out 'cos I find out if you stick together they can't get you out never mind what they say ('Jim', resident: 21–60).

Again, we have 'community' mobilised by this resident as a form of resistance and the protection of a sense of territory and belonging. Nonetheless, if we impute community to mean a wider social coherence, it rather crumbles in the face of the polarised opinions which surrounded the demolition plans. The older male focus group agreed that NDC was 'demolishing perfectly good houses'. Another individual older male respondent argued new houses were about 'yuppifying' the area and spoke of neighbours opposite his whose houses were being demolished, but were against it since they had lived there 'for 40 years and brought up families'. Similarly, the Youth Service organised a consultation between NDC and young people to discuss the redevelopment plans. According to one youth worker, the young people began the meeting saying new housing was a bad idea – people have lived there all their lives and so on. NDC staff countered this by offering a positive argument that it was the same community, just new houses. In response, one youth then asked, 'Will we have to buy them?' to which the NDC representative reportedly had no reply. Another youth worker claimed young people were, in general, 'not happy' at the plans, although none of the youths I interviewed mentioned the plans specifically, some even argued for better housing: 'We need new houses, the place looks like fucking Beirut' (Female resident: under 21). In the PA report, the initial consultation document upon which NDC was based, it clearly states that there was 'no great support for house building'. Moreover, the Neighbourhood Renewal Assessment of the Salford NDC states that there is 'no appetite for demolition, just renovation'. Nevertheless, there were some respondents who were either positive about the plans, or accepted them as a necessary step. For example: 'I think they are fantastic. I'd love to live in a riverside house, I've got no chance! [laughs] I'd love to live in one. Sit and listen to the river lapping at night? Ooh what! How can people disagree with that?' ('Jane', resident; 21–60).

Another older female resident 'Cath' said she could see why it is being done and is 'not bothered about it'. This may or may not have been because her (owner-occupied) house was unaffected by the plans, but she argued that the river was a good resource that should be utilised and the new houses would be 'nicer' and bring in more families to the area. She suggested that the area will be, 'nice when it is finished as long as they don't run out of money' ('Cath', resident: over 60). She continued by saying that many people were upset which she could understand, but it would be good for the area. The conflicting perspectives over the redevelopment plans were illustrated by the obstacles faced by those trying to organise resistance:

> All these houses here up to there, encompassing the old peoples home as well. Not here [points to row of 3 houses on the road front]. These people here don't even wanna live around here. You can't help that if they don't want to be helped. So we never took this on because they didn't want to know ... We did ask them and they said fuck off, couldn't get involved, didn't want to be involved ('Jim', resident: 21–60).

The contestation around redevelopment seemed to exacerbate a division between tenants and homeowners in their responses to the plans. For example, at one residents meeting, there was a report from a delegation who had attended a NDC physical environment task group, in hope of expressing resistance to demolition.

However, one of the 'delegates' reported that the NDC meeting had been dominated by homeowners with few tenants present, therefore there was little support for a 'non-owner' view on the plans. Perhaps unsurprisingly therefore and despite the evidence of collective resistance in some estates, it would be wrong to convey an impression of unity and agreement about the plans across the board. For example, an older female resident with close ties to the local Catholic church told me how in a specific estate, many people were angry at the way the plans were handled and were trying to form a new residents group to challenge and resist the plans. However, she made the point that many older people on the estate whom she knew, cannot get involved or do not want to get involved in the campaign. This point illustrates the caution required when considering the apparent 'community spirit' of such resistance. There will be a mixture of responses to such plans and differing levels of enthusiasm for 'fighting back'. Moreover, it was unclear how much of a lasting impact these examples of social capital would have beyond resisting the redevelopment plans. Was it an isolated example led by a small group of militant residents, or would it be a catalyst for a sustained commitment to the locality and 'ownership' of their neighbourhood? It seemed unlikely given the evident lack of agreement about the plans and the range of differing needs exhibited by residents.

Space Invaders

The final example of contestation within the NDC zone was around the presence of 'outsider' groups within the neighbourhood. There were three main groups about which data was generated – students, asylum seekers and private sector housing tenants. In general, the basis for this contestation was around claims on territory. Some of these contestations did manifest in actual real-life conflict over physical space, but there was a deeper level in which conflict appeared to be rooted; one where local residents feel, psychologically, that their space has been invaded, producing feelings of resentment or being threatened and so on, which was then expressed in ways that constructed such people or groups as a 'problem' or as 'other'. This process often took the form of social closure as documented by other studies of community dynamics and is a well-documented trend where there is mobility amongst residents or the existence of transitory populations.

If we consider students first, there is a large student community within the zone most of whom live within the halls of residence complex, safely contained within high walls, fencing and a 24-hour manned security entrance. Although some residents expressed no opinion on their presence and one was even positive about them, there was also a common perception of them as privileged, not contributing to or as a threat to 'their' community. For example, one residents group discussed how a part of their estate had been sold to the university who had used it to build student accommodation. They argued that this was 'destroying whole communities'. Similarly, a female resident had this to say:

See it used to be just student accommodation, but then when the students were on vacation, they let the flats off to different, other students from countries who want visit and you know, they come over and … But you've got all these gorgeous flats that have been built, specifically for students, I know they caused a terrible lot of resentment when they first went up ('Jane', resident: 21–60).

She also talked about the perceived lack of contribution made to the area by these incomers:

So, there is not a lot of money generated by people who come to university in Salford and when they've done the training, passed their degrees or what, they bugger off to their own places or where they've come from. Whether it be Leeds, Birmingham, Zimbabwe, wherever! So there is quite a lot of resentment towards students in Salford … are they offering anything to the community? I mean you get certain factions of universities who do, they go out of their way to promote good terms between themselves and you know, the people they're involved with. But then most people don't. They just go to their little bedsits at night, shut the door and that's it ('Jane', resident: 21–60).

Indeed, the students I spoke to largely did not see themselves as part of the community nor did they expect to. However, they did talk about the experiences and perceptions of the 'host' community: 'Yeah, I've heard stories of couple students going into the Prince of Wales [local pub] and after two pints they've said, 'yeah can you leave we don't want any trouble in here', so obviously landlords must know there was some hostility' ('Colin', student: under 21). Later the conversation returned to local pubs – communal spaces where both groups could interact:

M: Haven't met many of them [local people]. We got warned by the police not to go into any pubs round here so, probably I'd say no, they don't want us.

C: They don't have a problem saying "oh students this, students that", not that I've found. When I lived in Newcastle, it was all talk normally, but when they got to know you individually, they were alright really. I think it's just we get labelled as "we don't like students", but when they do meet you "oh you're alright". I think it's just a stigma attached. So when I've met people round here, usually in the betting shop, they're alright. They're like us in a way, they're sick of yobs round here more than owt.

The last comment highlights what could be the psychological or rhetorical process involved in labelling students as 'undeserving' residents whereas, in reality, relations are quite cordial. Nevertheless, there is evidence of explicit conflicts between students and local young people that will be explored further in the next section. Perhaps these conflicts might explain the bond that these students feel with some local (adult) residents, united in their dislike of 'yobs'. In the main however, students were seen as an alien presence, deserving of either exclusion from the community, or as targets for local misbehaviour. The PA report identified this insider /outsider division between the two groups, finding that many students do not feel 'part of the community'. This is to be expected, but their presence did induce unease or resentment in some residents and raised questions about what community NDC was aimed at and whether it could legitimately exclude students from the regeneration process.

The second group of 'space invaders' were refugees and asylum seekers. Media coverage of asylum and immigration has had many effects, but primarily it has helped politicise the issue to such an extent that it is inescapable when discussing community, particularly when a number of asylum seekers have been 'dispersed' to that locale. For example, a *Daily Express* article at the time (headline: The asylum seekers living in YOUR town) produced a list of the number of asylum seekers resident in each region in Britain (reference unknown). Across Salford as a whole, according to this report, there were 705 and, according to one local source, within the NDC zone itself, there were around 250 asylum seekers – only being 'dispersed' to the area in the previous two years. This development had introduced a racialised component to understanding community with a contrast between 'host' and immigrant populations identified, mapped and problematised. Within the zone, this group tend to be housed in one of two types of accommodation; privately run hostels, subsidised by the local authority, or private sector housing. Some respondents spoke compassionately about asylum seekers living in the area: 'I think round here, the majority do [accept them] because they don't cause anybody any bother. They keep themselves to themselves. I feel quite sorry for them at times' ('Jane', resident: 21–60, brackets added). Others acknowledged that there are some criteria for 'accepting' asylum seekers and that there is a feeling of animosity on the part of some:

> K: If they are coming over to work then it's ok.
>
> AW: People in this area, do they feel animosity towards asylum seekers?
>
> K: Yeah. They didn't at first when they first came because they felt sorry for them. But if they are just here to take advantage then ... ('Ken', resident: over 60).

Therefore, notions of deservingness come into play in understanding how community interacts with 'incomers'. A notion also advocated in the student interview:

> M: I just go with work. If they want to come and live in our country, you have to work. You can't just expect to live on benefits for the rest of their life as some of them do, you read the papers that they do, they're the people that wind me up ('Matt', student: under 21).

As with the student example, it appears, to an extent that perceptions of refugees tend to be bound up with popular discourses around work and 'contributing' to the community (cf. Dwyer 2000: 175). It is on this basis that they are 'othered', rather than due to direct experience of individual people or actual evidence of their 'scrounging'. Nevertheless, one resident did discuss actual conflict between the groups. He blamed any 'problems' on the local authority and their lack of foresight in how they handled the dispersal of asylum seekers in the area:

> Well, there is a problem with asylum seekers. They just put 'em in and they don't help them. They put 'em in and they expect people to get on ... I think what happens is they don't put one in and leave one, its five or six, seven or eight and I think people then feel intimidated and not in control of what's going on. So that causes problems ('Jim', resident: 21–60).

Therefore, there is an acknowledgement that there are problems, but in effect, it is not the fault of local people. 'Jim' went on to describe how local youths attacked a hostel that housed some refugees, but that they did so because they felt intimidated by large numbers of asylum seekers in their area:

> What happened is, one month there turned up 40, 50 Kosovan lads all 17–21, all in this building here and there was problems on the road with locals, there was conflict and then the next thing you know the local kids got a car, drove it through the doors, set the place on fire, while they were all in their basically. Next thing you know, apparently there was shots fired, all sorts of things. But that's cos, there was no consultation. People felt threatened because there was suddenly gangs of 10–15 Kosovans, Iraqis walking up the road, all single males, yeah? That's us there now [points]. These were all walking up the road causing problems – in gangs and I feel it was just too much at once ... that there [the building] has only got planning permission to be used for student accommodation. So what they did with these 40–50 Iraqi/Kosovan males they gave them all student cards for ManCat [local college] for English so that's how they got over it. But they weren't students – they didn't even go to college. But they got a card ('Jim', resident: 21–60).

It is unclear from this example whether refugees are being caught up in a wider struggle between local people and a supposedly unresponsive local authority, or if this issue of (non) consultation is an attempt by this resident to recast the 'asylum problem' into non-racist terms. What is clear is the gendered nature of this conflict. As 'Jim' states, it was men who were at the forefront of what was a territorial, not just racist dispute.

Some sympathy for the plight of asylum seekers was expressed at one residents meeting, with one person referring to the lack of support that they receive, although the majority of attendees rejected this sentiment claiming they get "teams of social workers". Another respondent confirmed that there had been some conflict produced by the location of refugees in the area:

> M: It's right in my view and in the view of local government and central government about the housing of asylum seekers and you very quickly get into the 'not in my back yard' scenario of 'yes we will have them, so long as they don't live here' and you've got to struggle with that issue and in some ways, force the issue through. Because they have to be housed somewhere.

> AW: Is that a thing that you have encountered?

> M: Yeah it certainly is around. Salford as a metropolitan authority, particularly the inner part of Salford is home to increasing numbers of asylum seekers and refugees and the New Deal area has taken its quota. 250 at the moment are in this area and erm, that is not without problem. Erm, we've had the backlash at times because of that. Because of who I am and the job that I do but also with the New Deal hat on, you feel you want to nip that in the bud and stand up to it straight away and actually say there are due processes through which we can deal with this and not through individuals taking it upon themselves to exclude (Local resident and partnership board member, 21–60).

Two NDC staff commented that the 'community' was initially very hostile to the presence of asylum seekers and that the culture of the area 'is very racist and 'old' Salford.' Several stories were recounted to me about incidents that occurred in the area where asylum seekers were victims of abuse and serious violence. This led one exasperated youth worker to wonder: 'Why can't Salford just turn around and say 'we don't want you'? They are welcomed and then abused' ('Jenny', youth worker: 21–60). Some local residents appeared to be mindful of being 'politically incorrect' when discussing asylum seekers, but the occasional comment did hint at distrust and an 'othering' process. Residents at one meeting conflated antisocial behaviour with 'people from other countries'. One older female respondent stated pejoratively that 'they' get 'lots' of asylum seekers and it is 'getting worse' because 'they died off, now they're back.'

Despite some obvious resentment and conflict with asylum seekers in the area, it would be unfair to characterise everyone in this light. The refugee support worker I interviewed argued that she believed 'host' residents over the age of forty or so try to be friendly and understand the issues facing refugees. This in contrast with a younger age group (teens to mid-twenties) that were hostile and more influenced by the tabloid media construction of asylum seekers as 'invaders' and 'freeloaders' and viewed them as a target. Nevertheless, there was a segment of the local population who considered asylum seekers to be 'space invaders'. This feeling was often expressed in connection with the perceived pernicious presence of private sector housing in the area, a sector that, for many people, produced many problems for the area and was sustained by the needs of asylum seekers as well as other problematic and transitory groups.

Within the NDC zone, privately rented housing was relatively common (11 per cent of all residents were private renters at the time according to CRESR 2003). There were patches of such houses scattered amongst the local authority housing, many of which were earmarked for demolition. The tenants of this housing tended to be constructed by other local residents as an undesirable presence in their community and as the main source of troublesome antisocial behaviour. For example:

> They've had a policy if you ask me of putting people on here who are bad tenants. At the top estate where me Dad lives, we don't have that problem because we don't have a high turnover, but down here it's been a high turnover and you find that most of tenants that they shove in here are not right. People with problems, or they've had problems on other estates, they've had 4 or 5 different houses, knock walls down then fuck off and go to another housing estate ('Jim', resident: 21–60).

The PA team reported that terraced housing residents were 'sick' of 'problem and nuisance people' in private rented houses and blamed them for some people 'here since birth' being forced to move away. Similarly, one resident's meeting discussed these 'bad' residents, blaming the 'riff raff' for the lack of demand for houses in a specific estate and its consequent demolition. There were references elsewhere to a 'bad' sort and 'problem families'. One older woman mentioned a high turnover of tenants in one estate, highlighting 'single mums' and 'immigrants', neither of whom stay long. Another resident identified a process whereby problematic council tenants move into the private sector:

> Well this woman had a camera in her house for the police to catch these people at the bottom of the street, they put her windows in. And that's what's gone on. So basically the problem that comes from the council is then pumped into here which is only round the corner from us. So there is ASBO's put on people they get kicked out there and come down here then ('Jim', resident: 21–60).

This movement from the public to the private sector was blamed, by one resident at a meeting, on unscrupulous property companies, arguing that they know they can rely on tenant welfare benefits to pay the rent. Private landlords came in for criticism generally for not vetting potential tenants and contributing to the perceived deterioration of some estates. The same older women claimed that they 'don't care who they let in'. She acknowledged that people 'have to live somewhere but I wouldn't like living amongst it.' Another resident emphasised this apparent negligent attitude: 'that's a private property company (points to sign), they couldn't give a shit about round here. He dumps whatever else shit in this area' ('Jim', resident: 21–60). This was supported by another respondent who argued that 'speculative landlords' are buying up a lot of properties: '[they let to] druggies and uh unruly kids you know with antisocial behaviour problems ... not actually on the estate where I live but round where there are these private landlords you see' ('Colin', resident: over 60). In support of this interview data, the PA team found a popular view amongst residents of private landlords being a major source of housing problems such as 'nuisance neighbours'. From interviews, it seemed clear that private tenants and the landlords that let to them were blamed for a variety of problems in the NDC zone. Such tenants were explicitly characterised not just as 'outsiders', but also as a threat to territory and behavioural norms. Of course, there is no merit in developing an apologist stance in relation to the problems that socially excluded residents face. That is, to ignore the fact that some residents will be a 'nuisance' or cause more problems than other people would be wilfully specious. However, it is unclear how much of a lawless threat these specific group of tenants are and, furthermore, whether they can be legitimately demonised or even criminalised in a homogeneous way. Herbert (2005) explored negative attitudes to renters on the part of homeowners in his study of Seattle, USA and suggested that it is part of a local politics geared towards defending property rights (p. 858). In my study however, it was a combination of homeowners and council tenants who were on the offensive. This may reflect a hierarchy of housing status where there is an active marginalising of those lacking the respectability afforded by stability and locality. In any case, the presence of private renters in areas like this will undermine, it would seem, any efforts to 'build community' (Herbert 2005: 858).

The purpose of giving these examples is to illustrate some of the processes involved in the contestation of community. This can take the form of conflicting needs or values (as with policing and redevelopment) or it can occur around the construction of insider/outsider groups within a geographical space. That is, in the process of doing community, some residents, deploying notions of 'belonging' and 'deservingness', actively construct divisions between groups, thus shaping the exclusion of their targets. Nevertheless, they are not simply passive victims in this process. It is difficult to argue that most university students for example, are socially excluded in any profound way, although they are excluded from membership of the community around them. Each 'space invader' group has opportunities to contest this process or will seek to manage it on their own terms. Examples included the young male staying at the homeless accommodation who avoids the local area or asylum seekers who, with the help of a local voluntary sector group, support each other because 'they are in the same boat' (refugee support worker). Social agents manage their exclusion in differing ways. The fundamental point is how the perceptions of some local people can have an impact on how incomers (but 'local' people nonetheless) experience that space. It seems some people are more local than others. This relational dimension to social exclusion will be further explored in Chapter 6.

Contestation of Space – Youth Shelters

This final section in the discussion of community argues that another dimension in its contestation is the struggle over the use of space within the neighbourhood. There was evidence from the field that illustrated how different groups with different needs clashed over the use of a space or facility within the NDC zone. This tended to happen either around regeneration plans (a conflict over how best to make use of physical space), or just a general conflict around spaces within the neighbourhood. The most explicit example of this was recounted to me by several sources including NDC staff, youth workers and young people. The PA team identified for NDC the possibility of a 'quick win'[3] project of youth shelters and a children's play area for which there appeared to be an appetite amongst residents. Young people in the area were included in the bidding and designing processes of these facilities but other local residents objected at the planning permission stage. Consequently, they were not built despite attempts to manage the conflict and develop a compromise. According to one youth worker, residents in the planned area feared the concentration of youths in one place and the related potential for trouble. The NDC voluntary sector support worker expressed it more bluntly: 'NIMBYism pure and simple. No one wanted it near them.' Some young people mentioned this conflict, but blamed NDC for not delivering on its promises ('NDC is shit. Said they'd give us youth shelter but it hasn't'). The implications of this type of contestation for tackling exclusion and promoting community will be explored later, but are indicative of a contradiction at the heart of NDC.

There were other similar examples whereby residents in other areas objected to the principle of play areas:

> We have got £50k per year to build parks, we've only built one in 3 years, and the reason they said they're no building anymore is because people don't want them. Because people don't understand what the parks are. This is a park, a nice fucking park … This is the sort of park we want on our estates, but because people thought "aw fucking climbing frames, do this, do that and whatever else", they all said "we don't want it outside the fucking house" – but we'd love one of these ('Jim', resident: 21–60).

In this example, the assumption about youth nuisance would have not only blocked a children's play space but also actually prevented one estate getting a 'nice' park. The NDC sector police sergeant commented on the difficulty this attitude creates:

> Up until recently they were adamant that they didn't want any facilities in the area for children. So they say "we're not having any facilities here, not in this area." And if you say to them "what should we do with them" "just move them".

---

3   'Quick win' refers to those potential short term, big impact projects that demonstrate to residents early on, that NDC is capable of delivering positive change.

So ideally, a lot of them want all the youths to be in their own home every hour of the day and the night and not come out onto the streets – which would be ideal. But unfortunately that doesn't happen and they've lost sight that when they were young that's what they did, they hung about the streets.

Young People and Public Space

This general conflict between young people and the rest of the community tended to manifest in various contestations of space. Another symbolic example was the local bowling green which some young males were using as a makeshift football pitch. The reason for which was explained thus:

> 'Cos this is how fucking mad it is round here. There's the football pitches for the kids and that's dogshit alley cos there's no fence round it, so they play on the bowling green, cos no-one uses the bowling green. So I said, put the fucking goal posts on here, so when these lads come, they play on here, they don't go over there, because if you notice that's what happens over there, everyone lets their dog go and they shit all over the football pitch (man lets his dog off leash to let it run). A bit of common sense, take them out there, put them on there, 'cos they still cut this grass ('Jim', resident: 21–60).

One young male confirmed this problem when he admitted that they play on the green because dog walkers use the pitch but that they 'get shouted at – we can't play anywhere'. However, a group of older men argued from their perspective, stating that they play bowls everyday but local schoolchildren did indeed use it for football, or as a dumping ground for wheelie bins as well as the occasional burnt out car. They asked NDC for bigger railings ('to keep kids out') but were refused. They told a story of a recent flashpoint whereby one of the older men physically removed a young male from the green and threatened to call the police. The young male responded, saying he would 'report' him to the police for manhandling him. The same youths then returned and let the tyres down on his car in retaliation. Other manifestations of this conflict include the police being called for young males playing football in a pub car park and complaints about the riding of motorbikes, not just around the estates, but also on the local playing fields. One residents group discussed the motorbikes issue at length and another resident mentioned them:

AW: Motorbikes are a big thing round here aren't they?

J: Oh god yeah! I know it's a terrible thing to say, but I've seen them come down and they're dodging all these cars coming up and the poor drivers that are coming up, it must be a nightmare for them, and I'm thinking, "I wish they'd hit the kerb" [laughs]. That's terrible ain't it?

AW: So, do they just drive around the streets?

J: Yeah. The noise is horrendous. Or down the back entries ('Jane', resident: 21–60).

One young male informed me that even when they ride the bikes on the playing fields, residents in the houses opposite phone the police and bikes are confiscated. A motorcycle track was suggested by another young male as a solution and the PA report also contained support for this suggestion, but at that time nothing had been planned.

The playing fields were another focal point for the contestation of space. The PA team found that burnt out cars are often dumped there and that this was an issue for many local people. I experienced this for myself. One evening in the walking through the neighbourhood accompanying 'detached' youth workers, we came across an incident where two cars had been burnt out and dumped on the playing fields. The police were already present at the scene, whilst another squad car chased another stolen car, this one with a caravan attached. The pursuit ended in the centre of a nearby estate and caused a sensation amongst local youths. The playing fields were used by young people as a place to congregate but were sealed off during that period for drainage in preparation for redevelopment into a sports complex. One young female protested that this deprived young people of somewhere to 'hang about' and would stop them having barbeques. The playing fields were also a site of conflict between young people, not just between youths and the adult population. One young male (aged 14, so younger than most other respondents) mentioned that the playing fields were always full of bikes and cars and that young males from other estates in the NDC zone stole their bikes.

Conflict over space between youths was also identified by young males in another area of the NDC zone, which had had a new play area built, including a swing park and a multi-purpose facility for football, basketball and netball. One 17-year-old male said older residents 'tell him off' if he is in the play area whilst the police moved his friend on. Two younger males (in their early teens) described how they could not use the new sports facility because 'older lads' from another estate drink alcohol on it at nights. It is this kind of data that throws up questions about the actual effectiveness of regeneration (in the sense of improving or introducing facilities) when it is mediated by this level of conflicting social relations.

Other Contestations of Physical Space

Some other examples of a contestation of space in the area included the presence of a pupil referral unit in the NDC zone. An empty school was being used for children with behavioural difficulties and produced some conflict with local young people as well as anger from residents who objected to its existence:

Now this school here has been empty for a while then they used it as a pupil referral unit – 35 kids we had in it. Basically it brought the area right down … the police were there in the morning to see them going in, they were there at break time in case they jumped over the fucking fence. They were there in the afternoons when they went for their dinner, they were there at night time, and they used to bus these kids in and out. But there was without a doubt, we'd find cars in the park every night the kids in the area used to get intimidated by them … Now New Deal own that building so I says to New Deal, we own that building – we'd already petitioned them with 680 petitions, we did that in a week, we got 600 names on a petition saying we don't want it using as a sin bin …at the end of the day if you're going to build something like that you've got to take everybody's community into account. And the only way to do it really is put it out the area, bus them all in, bus them all out, because no-one wants it. Simple ('Jim', resident: 21–60).

Another incident was isolated to a specific part of the NDC zone, where one estate bordered a traveller's caravan site. At the local residents meeting, there was intense discussion about conflict with this group who they claimed were dumping rubbish on the estate rather than the nearby 'official' dumping site. Fly tipping was a problem generally, but travellers were the only ones to be blamed as a group (see Kenrick and Bakewell 1990 for an account of a similar conflict between gypsies and local residents).

Conclusion

The data cited here about contestations of community encompasses a range of aspects including the conflicts over physical space and facilities, conflicts rooted in differing needs and values and an 'othering' of 'outsider' groups within the neighbourhood. These combine to produce a space that is patterned and stratified by a range of social divisions which shape and are shaped by how individuals experience and 'do' community. Another important point of this chapter has been to illustrate that stratification can be done by agents. That is, the way community and exclusion is experienced is partly shaped by the social relations that residents participate in and negotiate. This analysis of how community (dis)functions has significant implications for how we understand NDC to be addressing the social exclusion of poor citizens by constituting them through and binding them to particular social-political configurations that prioritise cohesion, local identity and of course active agency. It is to this latter factor that we now turn.

Chapter 5

Another 'Urban Snatch'?

Introduction

This chapter is a further examination of the key concepts of community, agency and exclusion deemed to underpin the NDC programme. Allied to the discussion in the previous chapter which problematised the model of community that infused the NDC regeneration approach, here I offer a critical analysis of how New Labour – through NDC – understood and enacted the role and capacity of individual citizens in poor neighbourhoods. As I have asserted, regeneration through community was valorised through the imputation of an active, engaged resident population. This constituted a responsible citizenry bound to particular social formations underpinned by spatiality with a corresponding identity, sense of belonging and aspirational scope. After providing an account of NDC and the role of individual agency in regenerating communities as well as the role of regenerated communities in constructing agency, this chapter examines some of the literature that unsettles the assumptions that underpinned the relationship between local residents and the NDC regeneration experience. It then compliments this discussion by citing evidence from my field research which generated some important questions about the capacity and willingness of NDC residents to participate in and validate the regeneration and governance of both their neighbourhood and their citizenship.

New Labour, NDC and Agency

Closely related to the model of community outlined in Chapter 4 is the conception of agency that underpinned NDC and infused the new spaces of governance which NDC and its residents inhabited. Again, there were two key dimensions to this model. Firstly, there was a belief that NDC neighbourhoods contained a priori, individual social agents that were able and willing to fulfil their civic responsibilities (defined by Government) within their community (again, defined by Government) by virtue of their 'strong sense of identity and shared aspirations' (NRU 2001: 8). All that was required were effective methods of consultation and inclusive avenues of participation to yield active forms of individual agency. In the context of NDC, these responsibilities referred to an engagement with the ongoing practice of the programme by supplying ideas and analyses of local problems and their solutions, attending NDC meetings and perhaps devising and managing service development projects, funded by NDC and designed for local residents. More generally, they referred to an emotional commitment to the community in which civic responsibility and kinship with other residents was to be felt and practiced, thereby bolstering local social capital whilst enabling residents to draw on their localism to challenge the established political and policy structures that framed their (local) citizenship.

There was also a normative dimension whereby expected forms of behaviour were promoted and instilled by NDC and the resultant 'active' community. The first step was the construction of a community through NDC in which residents were expected to participate. Part of NDC's remit involved stimulating that participation in specific ways, such as facilitating residents to attend community meetings, stand for election to the NDC board, or organise and 'own' local services. This was consistent with New Labour's acknowledgment that regeneration programmes must prioritise the participation of local residents and derived from 'the theory and practice of community development where participation, empowerment and ownership are seen as necessary conditions for change' (Dinham 2005: 302). However, it went further than being a motor of local change because New Labour appeared to believe in the positive effect of participation per se. They did consider its importance in achieving sustainable regeneration but also contended that involvement in one's community was a civic responsibility requiring no further justification from government and indeed, would encounter little resistance from eager citizens (see Blears 2003). This was in line with their belief that community was also about according opportunities for individuals to develop 'enlightened self interest' (Deacon 1998) which benefits them and their communities.

As noted in the discussion of community, another form of resident action NDC sought to stimulate was to encourage residents to make claims on the behaviour of other residents via NDC's consultation process. This embodied a definite notion of community as a functioning moral framework wherein behaviour could be mapped, challenged and regulated. NDC was a way in which 'decent' citizens could 'take a stand' against antisocial behaviour and incivility (Home Office 2003). More broadly – if we consider the quote below – NDC was also about appeasing sceptical taxpayers by invoking a principle of conditionality (Dwyer 1998) that made spending on 'renovating' 'problem' estates conditional on 'good' behaviour:

> We are not going to put taxpayers money into inner city redevelopment unless as a partnership which involves something for something ... we are renovating estates but making clear that we will act when tenants behave unacceptably ... we do not tolerate anti-social behaviour or lawlessness. We will put in the police and the laws to stamp it out (Blair 2001).

Consequently, NDC became a 'deal' between subaltern places and the state in which resources were delivered, but on condition that subject populations police themselves adequately and manage the (assumed negative) behaviour of residents. NDC facilitated that policing process and was a mechanism through which the moralising, 'active' community voice could be expressed. Again, we have a dual model, this time of agency; one that presumes a level of consensus about social norms and values amongst residents that can be harnessed to support an intervention like NDC, hence its 'rewarding' with NDC status. However, it is also a model that has a firm belief in how agents should act and behave. That is, it promotes forms of social action deemed necessary and 'responsible', encompassing participation in civic life and the judgement of others. The emphasis placed on public participation straddles both of these dimensions in that it is deemed necessary to provide a platform for the former in addition to encouraging the latter.

Questioning Agency

Chapter 2 stressed the centrality of notions of 'responsibility' and good character to New Labour's reform of welfare and redefinition of the citizen-state relationship. In the context of NDC this was translated into a model of agency which encompassed a set of responsibilities and behaviours expected of and cultivated in NDC residents. There are a number of points to address about this model. Firstly, as touched on in the discussions of welfare reform there was a general ongoing debate about New Labour's attempt to foreground the behaviour and character of citizens, particularly when used to retrench welfare rights (Dwyer 1998) and when subject to increased surveillance and behavioural scrutiny across a range of contexts (Clarke 2005). Much of the debate questions the Giddensian analysis of the need for 'autotelic' citizens who can reflexively respond to the risks and uncertainties of this historical epoch, whether described as late or post modern, post-traditional or post-Fordist (e.g. Mann 2003). Some also expressed concern about the apparent uneven application of behavioural expectations. That is, to reiterate Dwyer's point, it is social welfare (as opposed to fiscal or occupational welfare) recipients who have seen greater scrutiny of their conduct (1998: 514).

Much of the debate around NDC derives from the sort of analysis similar to that around welfare reform in general. For instance, the responsibility placed on residents to be responsive, active agents who drive social change in their communities stems from the same model of responsible agency as propounded by Giddens and the 'third way'. This model throws up some interesting questions about New Labour's communities as inhabited by both consensual and reflexive, transformative social agents. Presumably, New Labour believed residents of NDC zones exercised reflexivity in the same, that is, consensual way. Nevertheless, the questions we can ask of the 'responsibilisation' of citizens in a regeneration context are twofold (and can broadly be applied to Giddens' view of post-traditional agency). Firstly, why should residents want or have to participate in their own governance? As Marinetto (2003) has recently pondered 'who wants to be an active citizen?' As we have seen, in NDC areas residents are expected, and assumed to want to engage in the regeneration of that space. To some extent, participation is implicitly demanded by the construction of the area as a 'New Deal' community with the emphasis placed on local involvement as a prerequisite for sustainable renewal.

In his article, Marinetto cites a Foucauldian governmental perspective to suggest that such demands of active citizenship and 'community involvement' could be a strategy of government designed to regulate the population: 'encouraging active citizenship promotes a particular type of personal morality and positive forms of life for communities, individuals and families' (2003: 109). Similarly, Nikolas Rose, an advocate of a broadly similar Foucauldian approach argues that the use of community to underpin active, participative citizenship is about shaping individual behaviour by inscribing: 'the norms of self control more deeply into the soul of each citizen than is thought possible through either disciplinary technologies such as mass schooling or social technologies such as those of welfare states' (Rose 2000: 1409). However, Marinetto notes that such a perspective, given its contention that governing and disciplinary power is dispersed throughout society, perhaps fails to consider the role of centralised government power in defining meanings of citizenship and its attendant responsibilities (2003: 110). In turn, this allows us to consider the moralism which shaped much of New Labour welfare agenda (Deacon and Mann 1997). That is, New Labour was unequivocal about its scrutiny of behaviour from the centre and clearly considered it an electoral boon to appear 'tough', as well as an avenue for reshaping the social.

Nevertheless, it was Giddens' reflexive subject that New Labour seemed to support (Greener 2002: 693) and made manifest through programmes such as NDC. This was a model of agency consistent with a political rationality that Rose argues took shape in pre-war Britain as 'the citizen' became:

> A social being whose powers and obligations were articulated in the language of social responsibilities and collective solidarities ... Citizens should want to regulate their conduct and existence for their own welfare, that of their families and that of society as a whole (1999: 228).

There are shades here of the 'autotelic' self and the belief that individuals should seek to negotiate challenges and take responsibility for their behaviour. A belief that as Mann notes, is redolent of 'Victorian ideas of self help' (2003: 230), with increasing responsibilities on citizens but, crucially, without an analysis of the configuration of risks shaped by social and welfare divisions. As Fitzpatrick puts it:

> Their [Giddens and Beck] vision of the reflexive agent is ... a self unconstituted by political conflict, of an environment from which hegemonic struggle has been all but eliminated and where grand questions concerning the justice or injustice of social background conditions are much less relevant than before (2005b: 58, brackets added).

If one were to apply this critique to NDC, one would contrast the awareness of self and commitment to community that NDC was meant to both feed off and inculcate, with the structural context in which this formulation of agency is supposed to occur. That is, a context of consistent disadvantage, conditions of social exclusion or poverty in addition to a culture of distrust of the state which raises questions about the propriety of expecting residents to be either willing or able to get involved in local governance and be dynamic agents of social change. Alcock has analysed this trend in social policy towards 'agency based social change' and suggested that it could amount to the 'pathologisation' of the 'social exclusion problem' and the re-emergence of a 'victim blaming' policy model. He states: 'the insistence on local solutions to local problems can suggest that all such problems and solutions are locally based ... [and] may lead some national (or international) actors to assume that they have no role to play in these' (2004: 93–4). The reframing of urban regeneration as being shaped from the 'bottom up' rests on getting local citizens involved and risks underplaying structural determinants. Here we can adopt Hoggett's analysis of Giddens' understanding of agency to question this reframing process. He suggests that Giddens' understanding derives from a 'traditional critique of the so-called 'dependency culture' and argues that his analysis lacks, 'any sense of power, domination, oppression, capitalism, imperialism, racism, etc. which might help us understand why poor people are as they are' (2000: 5). The outcome of such inadequate analyses is a model of the self that masquerades as the solution to the onset of post-traditional risks, but actually fails to reflect the processes by which social experience is produced. It is possible to see a resemblance here with how NDC constructs its residents. Furthermore, Mann suggests that Giddens' model is 'an individualistic agenda that blames the poorest for not being more like the middle classes' (2003: 238). He suggests that not only should the inadequacies of the model be revealed as lacking structural context, but the concepts of reflexivity and the 'autotelic' self are imbued with an implicit class bias, and Giddens' apparently universal ideas about 'self help' are actually bourgeois conceits. As Mann notes: 'The suspicion remains though that the discovery of the autotelic self is lower down the agenda of the people of Essex than the restoration of fiscal welfare measures such as MIRAS' (1998: 93). Consequently, New Labour's reliance on 'community involvement' and active agency to sustain regeneration not only raised concerns about its neglect of structural impediments to engaged and responsive residents, but could reflected a lack of subtlety in its understanding of human agency. For example, as with Giddens, there was an emphasis on emboldened, reflexive, engaged citizens. However:

> There is something slightly compulsive about a subject which constantly seeks to be stretched and tested ... the fact is that we are also natural and corporeal beings, we have bodies which do cause us suffering (and more suffering for some than for others) and which do decay and die. Western culture, and North American culture in particular, often seems to be in flight from an acceptance of the limits that nature provides (Hoggett 2001: 43–4).

Hoggett called for a holistic model of agency, one that recognised the 'fractured self' and the 'impact of fear, envy and other emotions upon our capacities to imagine, challenge, resist or lead' (2000: 12). Elsewhere, he described this as a 'non-unitarist' model of agency that recognises the 'negative emotional capabilities' of individuals and 'the capacity for self-destructiveness and destructiveness towards others' (2001: 53). Indeed, in the previous chapter we saw how these 'negative capabilities' can manifest in destructive relationships with fellow community members and contest the social fabric that allegedly should exist between fellow residents. It is at this point that we can broaden our analysis of the conflicts and divisions described in Chapter 4. These are significant not just because they reflect a lack of cohesion or togetherness within a particular neighbourhood, but that these divisions often have a basis in experiences of poverty and disadvantage which play out, for example, in frustrations over a lack of 'legitimate' public space to occupy or the presence of 'outsider' groups.

Hoggett's analysis of agency offers an alternative, more nuanced understanding of human behaviour and, I would argue, problematises New Labour's focus on active, responsible, respectable citizens as both a policy output and a validation for its community project. The communities of the New Labour imagination were rather sterile projections that lacked a grounding in the realities of excluded spaces where, like other spatial entities, residents can be in conflict and behave in ways, perhaps not accounted for by New Labour, but no less human for that. If we want to try and define the essence of community, perhaps it could be that its potential 'leakiness' (Newman and Clarke 2009), disorder, even dysfunctionality are 'natural' aspects which should not automatically place them outside the scope of the regeneration arena. Furthermore, these facets of community invite us to consider how residents experience, react to and shape the spaces of governance they are increasingly drawn into. This is not to deny that individual and collective citizens can participate in their own governance successfully, but to illuminate and explore how they do so within anaemic understandings of community, agency and exclusion coupled with expectations that they should and must participate effectively. It would appear that citizenship governance has become a duty owed, a repayment for generous government-financed 'opportunities' and concerns remain that it ensnares citizens in a nexus of political activism that compounds rather than helps to ameliorate their disadvantage.

Activated Citizens – Who Participated in NDC?

The NDC process was kick-started by a neighbourhood-wide consultation conducted by a participatory appraisal (PA) team. The team included three 'community animators' who were also residents and made use of innovative research techniques to ensure that as many local people were consulted as possible about what they would like from NDC, how the area could be improved and so on. The results of this audit were translated into the 'PA report' and used as a key bidding document for NDC funding (designed to illustrate to central Government the efforts made to engage residents). Indeed the PA methodology was commended by central Government in their first annual review of NDC (NRU 2001: 14). However, two NDC staff I interviewed were less impressed, arguing that the PA process had been conducted in such a manner that it raised unrealistic hopes on the part of residents that have so far not been met. This has led to widespread disillusion at a relatively early stage in the programme's lifespan. One community representative I spoke to confirmed this feeling:

> But what has actually happened since then, there has been so much consultation particularly using sticky dots on flip charts and post it notes and no real results from the consultation, local people are now saying they feel over-consulted and they are not prepared to be consulted any more[1] ... What they are upset about is the fact that there was so much given to PA, and you know, it was sold as we want to hear what you want ... So, they basically feel they have been promised the earth and they have not been given anything and they are angry about it and I don't blame them ('Bill', resident and community representative: 21–60).

Indeed, there has been recent revision of the PA method with one of the lessons learned from the Salford experience being that it 'runs the risk of raising expectations'. Furthermore, it has been learned that what is required in a regeneration context is 'ongoing information to the local community, agencies and other stakeholders about the scope, duration and steps required in implementing PA' (Oxfam 2005). In Salford, communication with residents about the consultation process did not seem to have taken place thus creating a gap in understandings of the reality of PA and what it could realistically achieve.

Nevertheless, there was substantial consultation of residents from the beginning and the PA team became the Community Involvement Team (CIT) with a remit to improve community involvement in and awareness of ongoing NDC projects. This was the first method designed to 'strengthen' the community – to produce a report based on wide consultation, which translated individual needs and values into a community agenda for change and improvement.

The most elementary means by which I attempted to explore the efficacy of NDC's model of the active resident was obviously to examine the extent of engagement, amongst residents, with the NDC process as well as non-NDC organisations – those that can loosely be judged to be part of the fabric of the neighbourhood. That is, what level of attachment to the NDC area could be discerned and what level of attachment to fellow NDC residents? The key concepts of 'interest' and 'involvement' were the basis for data generation, deployed to question directly the assumptions contained within New Labour's model of agency.

NDC business appeared to be a relatively transparent process in Salford with residents encouraged to participate through poster campaigns, newsletters

---

1 'Bill' was referring to what he saw as the emptying of meaning of consultation, which, if not backed up by visible changes becomes an irritation, rather than an avenue of self-determination.

and through electing their community representatives. The key mechanisms of participation were the six task groups that met every month to discuss one of the six themes of regeneration such as crime, education, physical environment and how to build community. These meetings were open to the public and were an avenue through which residents could voice opinions and objections about NDC projects and plans. Furthermore, local people could attend the NDC community forum (doubling as the local authority community committee) and were free to engage with council officers and attending NDC community representatives. Moreover, resident nominations to the governing partnership board were made through this forum. These representatives were directly elected for a year by those who attended the committee meeting (there were six residents present at my meeting in addition to Council officers and so on). One community representative I spoke to admitted this process of election was far from ideal:

> So you've got a Council committee that becomes a community forum and it means that the people who can vote are members of community committee, they are the only ones who can vote for community reps ... So, the reality is that something like 17 people elect the community reps for NDC. Which I've argued all along very strongly excludes 99% of the population from that electoral process ('Bill', resident: 21–60 and NDC community representative).

The partnership board met in private, but contained six community representatives and was chaired by a local resident to ensure adequate representation. In the course of undertaking my fieldwork, I attended both the local community committee and the 'Building Communities' task group. The 'Building Communities' programme was responsible for debating and organising the community involvement agenda of NDC. However, on the occasion of my visit, only two residents attended, both of which were active NDC stakeholders – one community representative and the other a paid employee in NDC's community involvement team (CIT). At that time, she was the only local person actually employed by NDC, a sore point for some residents I interviewed. For example,

> ... that's the way they are down there at New Deal. It's them and us and the reason is, we used to have 4 community involvement workers who lived in the area. We've got one now. We've got one person who works for New Deal who lives in the area, out of a staff of 30. New Deal are meant to employ from within ... And where are we? Why aren't we working there, why aren't we the outreach workers, why aren't local people ... 'Jon' who lives there [points], he went for the job and got fucked off and they employed someone from out the area who sits on her arse and we don't even see her ('Jim', resident: 21–60).

It appeared in my experience of meetings and of talking to residents in general, that most felt excluded from the NDC process despite its transparency and apparent accessibility. For example, the 2003 Performance Management report

(Charlestown and Lower Kersal NDC Partnership 2003a) found that despite crime being the biggest issue for local people, few residents attended the relevant task group (2003a: 15). Moreover, it found a local resident chaired only one out of six task groups (2003a: 31). Meetings appeared very poorly attended and those who did attend could be identified as a select few determined community actors who dominated channels of involvement. One community representative and consistent presence at meetings felt under pressure due to this wider non-participation saying she felt 'like a one man band'.[2] Another lamented this lack of engagement,

> It's about it [community inclusion] yeah. But it's not doing it. It's not achieving it. We've still got, we've got 6 focus [task] groups: in Building Communities I am probably the only person who lives in the area who is involved with it. Children and young persons, I don't think there is anyone in the area involved in it; education employment and skills, you tend to get one person there. Crime you get a few; physical environment you get quite a few; but they're really the only ones ('Bill', resident and community representative: 21–60, detail added).

In Salford, this seemed indicative of a wider culture of disengagement that pervaded the relationship between the individual and (local) state. Indeed, the 2005 annual report for Salford NDC showed that the number of residents who had even heard of NDC was still only 82 per cent of those surveyed (although up from 63 per cent in 2002) (Charlestown and Lower Kersal NDC Partnership 2005: 5), meaning there were around at least 1,800 residents who were not aware of the programme even after four years. Moreover, there existed a degree of suspicion around NDC due to its close ties with the local authority, some disillusionment due to the slow pace of change and consultation fatigue and some outright hostility most often expressed in relation to the housing redevelopment plans. However, when it came to understanding the poor levels of involvement, the chairperson of the partnership board, also a resident, was clear where she felt the responsibility lay:

> I suppose more could be done, but what do you do more? You've got a newsletter that comes out, people are told where meetings are, time of meetings have been changed from afternoon to evenings back to afternoons. We've had various events where information is given out. The community committee meets every two months and updates are given on NDC. But, you could never employ enough people to do enough door knocking and go around and meet with people. I mean, like I say information is put out, information is produced. All the meetings are open, anybody can attend. I think it's just the way of the world unless it affects

---

2 A community worker interviewed also identified this phenomenon fearing that those influential local actors who dominate now, would dominate any post-NDC community organisation, thus obscuring the potential empowerment of less influential local people. This is a common problem for local participation. See, for example, Marilyn Taylor (2000).

you, that little bit where you live, you don't actually get your bum into action do you? ('Mary', resident and chair of NDC partnership board: 21–60).

Her view was that people tended not to be able to see beyond their own immediate interests and therefore found it difficult to engage with long term, perhaps more mundane NDC business. A more circumspect analysis of resident apathy was offered by the NDC voluntary sector support worker who identified a disconnect that was rooted in a sense of distrust of local government with which NDC was regularly conflated and general poor community infrastructure on top of which NDC was imposed. Moreover, these factors could have been exacerbated by inadequate participatory mechanisms, contrary to what 'Mary' argues above. For example, the local NDC Performance Management report concluded that: 'NDC has structural weakness with a lack of strong community involvement … [and] opportunities to engage at a local level [are] not always taken' (Charlestown and Lower Kersal NDC Partnership 2003a: 30, brackets added). 'Mary's' analysis also neglects to consider the nature and content of NDC meetings, which for many may appeared 'aloof' and 'full of suits' (Female community worker). Indeed, these negative perceptions of NDC meetings are echoed in Dinham's (2005) study of resident views in a London NDC area. Certainly, the quote above and the community committee meeting I attended are examples of the disconnection between residents and officials. When local people made complaints to council officers, they were largely ignored or they could not respond satisfactorily. The two groups seemed to talk past each other, both with different perceptions about the purpose of the meeting. Another factor was the often fractious atmosphere of such meetings. Arguments could be personality driven and revolve around obscure details about funding arrangements of community groups and so on. Added to this, the structure of elected (although their mandate is negligible) community representatives was questioned by the voluntary sector support worker who lamented that most community representatives are 'in it for themselves', that there is little feedback to and from communities and they use meetings as a chance to 'have a go at council people rather than be productive.' Considering all these factors it was perhaps unsurprising that residents were reluctant to engage with the rather arcane practices of a regeneration programme and that it only attracted, for the most part, those more determined and motivated community actors. Consequently, I got a definite sense from respondents and meetings, of NDC and the community co-existing in the same space, but on parallel plains, rarely intersecting. It was difficult to envisage how existing structures of participation and community involvement would produce the desired outcomes of a stronger community (beyond the elite set of dominant voices). At this stage in the NDC process, it seemed that residents felt both over exposed to participation techniques ('too many sticky dots on charts' as one respondent wryly noted), but felt excluded from 'real' involvement with NDC or did not perceive their sticky dots to be having an impact.

Salford City Council and NDC

> They know it's not right – the remit is New Deal for Communities and it's New
> Deal for councils here in a big way ('Jim', resident: 21–60).

One of the recurring themes when interviewing both NDC staff and some residents
was the criticism made of the local Labour-controlled city council. NDC was an
independent partnership with its own funding stream, intended to be additional to
mainstream budgets. However, the local authority were the accountable body for
NDC finances, there were council staff working for NDC and local councillors sat
on the partnership board. None of this is particularly unreasonable or suspect but it
seemed to strain the relationship between the two organisations. The NDC deputy
co-ordinator described the council as 'very paternalistic and difficult'. A resident
and community representative echoed this point:

> I said from the start that it was a culture shock for the council. Because they
> have never been used to working in partnership. They're used to being in control
> and they're used to exercising power and I recognised that they had a genuine
> problem. They had to let go of power and nobody wants to do that. Especially
> when they have gone into to some form of government which is about exercising
> control and exercising power and all the rest of it ('Bill', resident: 21–60).

This theme came up in another interview with NDC staff. One programme manager
described a picture of local governance where 'old Labour paternalism' was 'rife'
and argued that the local authority 'go along with NDC reluctantly' because they
see it as 'another pot of cash to be doled out', rather than a 'partnership' between
state, voluntary sector and the community. In their view, it was the 'culture' of the
local authority that was a key barrier to NDC succeeding because of entrenched
opposition to communities exercising greater control over resource allocation
and decision-making – precisely the core agenda of NDC in the eyes of staff and
stakeholders and the necessary prerequisite to 'sustainable' regeneration. This
reflected research conducted by Aspden and Birch (2005) who found that in some
local partnership areas, local councillors exhibited wariness about the involvement
of voluntary and community groups in local decision-making. They argued that
such levels of involvement challenge councillors' self-image as 'legitimate and
accountable community leaders and representatives' (cited in Ellison and Ellison
2006: 341).

Conversely however, some respondents spoke about a culture amongst
residents that supported the local council's alleged paternalism. A partnership
board member and local resident 'Gary' made this point:

> One of the things this community is not good at, it is impoverished at participating
> in the life of the city. People do not join in on the life of their city on all fronts,
> they don't feel able to. It's a real paternal relationship you know, the old style,

people do things for us, and the enormous challenge is making people more participatory.

The NDC deputy co-ordinator was more forthright, talking about a 'dependency culture' in the area. She described the culture as one that engendered a lack of 'taking responsibility' amongst residents. This was a theme she returned to several times by way of explaining what she envisaged as NDC's role and purpose in the community: 'about trying to get away from paternalism towards community governance and ownership of new facilities.' For her, NDC was designed to disrupt traditional models of governance and service delivery by promoting and activating the local community and drawing them in as partners. Therefore, social exclusion was as much about a lack of input and ownership of local services and facilities, as a lack of resources and diminished life chances and the best way to halt the decline was to galvanise local people into procuring a stake in their community. She implied that a 'dependency culture' was damaging in its effects, in that it was a social malaise whereby residents are unwilling or unable to challenge their own conditions of exclusion, they resent the authority upon which they are dependent whilst 'regeneration' will be superficial and unsustainable. She cited an example of a new health centre in the area, partly financed by NDC to illustrate her point about the importance of 'ownership'. She argued that there had to be a sense of ownership amongst residents and pointed out the futility of investing in it if it is then 'torched and barricaded' by local people. She drew an interesting parallel with the sense of ownership felt about the local sports facilities owned by an illustrious professional soccer club, which were 'untouched' and apparently free from the threat of serious vandalism.

The idea of a 'dependency culture' in the area was a recurrent theme among several respondents, particularly those who worked in the area (such as NDC and community and youth workers).[3] This led to some discussions about how the culture should be changed with NDC leading that change:

> If, at the end of the partnership, after ten years we actually haven't strengthened the community so that they have community leaders and more people generally throughout the community who have the confidence and skills to get on with their own lives and through the organisations and volunteering etc. I think that will be one of the ways we can say New Deal has failed … I am not wanting to make these people middle class, but want to give them the confidence that they can play a … that you know, just because the city council says it is going to happen, doesn't mean you can't change it. Historically they have not had those skills because constantly they have been disabled by process ('Gary', local resident and partnership board member: 21–60).

---

3   The term 'dependency culture' was implied rather than spoken by most respondents. It is unclear how the perception of such a culture grew amongst staff and practitioners.

This resident argued that inadequate systems of participation and a lack of a commitment to boosting community identity had produced a weak sense of entitlement and identification prevalent amongst excluded people. He cited NDC as an opportunity to challenge this trend by strengthening a community sense. It was through this concept of a 'strong community' that individuals confidence and skills could be developed and the malignant 'dependency culture' overcome. This resembles the normative aspect of NDC's model of individual agency explored above which promoted agents' involvement in their community: a sentiment partly rooted in a moralising agenda aimed at improving individual behaviour, but also at responsibilising forms of state-directed governance (Hastings 2003: 99). That is, only properly empowered local actors can challenge the dominance of the local council and avoid the perceived neglect of poor neighbourhoods by self-interested or disinterested politicians and bureaucrats. The dispersal of governance therefore appeared to depend on the capacity of citizens to participate effectively in policy spaces and challenge and contest established working patterns and relations of power between governing and governed.

Another respondent argued that NDC was less about changing individual behaviour and more about installing more formal structures to sustain the improvement of the area by bolstering the community infrastructure, thus avoiding a reversion back to relying upon 'old' styles of governance:

> So the other thing that I am pushing for and have been pushing for, for about 18 months to 2 years looking to the future, I want a community development trust so we can maintain the partnerships that we've developed but we can have a legacy that can give us an income in order to sustain what we've got and develop it further. And that for me is how New Deal can become sustainable, otherwise we get to 2010, the money runs out and 'bye bye'. It just becomes another regeneration initiative and unless you get that continuity, it falls down. So that's what I've been pushing for ('Bill', resident and community representative: 21–60).

To return to the supposed paternalism of the local authority, there are implications for the reported over weaning council influence – the perception that the council, because of its inherent paternalism and apparent reluctance to renounce some of its power, tried to influence the NDC process to control the allocation of resources. There was a perception amongst some that the council has too great a presence on the partnership board, a sentiment that seemed to be rooted in a deep sense of distrust and dissatisfaction with local government generally. As one resident noted after the first NDC community animation (a survey of resident opinions and needs): 'We had to work quite hard at first to explain that we weren't the DSS in disguise. The words New Deal certainly confused people!' ('Phil', resident and community animator, cited in NRU 2001: 15). It is difficult to assess how well founded these perceptions were. Certainly, the partnership board, the body that took key decisions and oversaw the effective delivery and management of the NDC programme, did contain three local councillors, alongside residents and individuals from other agencies. Moreover, it is a fact that the local authority managed NDC finances,

> ... it takes months and months and months and months to get anything done because the council's the accountable body and so you have to follow their processes. So everything has to be agreed by the appropriate member of the council, you have to follow the council's tender processes and it takes months to get anything done. And it can take months to get cheques issued. We've got community chest which is the source of funding for the groups and you could succeed in an application and wait two or three months for the cheque to come through from civic centre. A total nonsense ('Bill', resident and community representative: 21–60).

For some, this was an influence that not only slowed progress, but also illustrated something more sinister at play: 'But that meant that everyone who works for New Deal works for the council. So they can't represent us and the council. They are all on council contracts of employment.' ('Jim', resident: 21–60) 'Jim' went on to tell me:

> ... because we had apathy in this area and no one got involved right, they [the council] just took over. I'm sorry to say but it's the way we are in Salford, we've had that many bad dealings with the councils, they ask us why we don't come to meetings 'cos ... you sit there for 2 or 3 hours to talk about base targets blah blah blah. Then someone gets up and says "me gas isn't fucking working" and they say, "oh you can't come for individual things", well what the fuck are we coming here for then. You know, we've come here because we're getting no joy down there and you're the boss so you sort it out ... But when the money came in this area, the council knew what to do, started moulding it the way they wanted it because we've always suffered this apathy or this non-involvement because we've always been the way we have. Any council, any authority because we've been shit on for years and years, so you know, they ask why don't you get involved, what's the fucking point? You don't listen to us anyway when we got involved ('Jim', resident: 21–60, brackets added).

A further dimension to this relationship between NDC and local council was that this apparent political influence distorted the analysis of need within the zone. Local politicians insisted on the problematic identification of two distinct wards as a community for political ends and in spite of obvious and documented socioeconomic differences between the two wards that comprise the zone:

> ... there are different strata of society within the area, there are some parts quite wealthy and some parts certainly not wealthy at all. There is a political divide between the two wards ... what one ward gets, the other expects to get and you get a lot of dissent between the two ... But there is this political insistence that

they are both the same, homogeneous and it should be split down the middle in effect but in reality the need is one sided ('Bill', resident and community representative: 21–60).

Therefore, the ability of NDC to challenge the exclusion of people in a way that met their needs was compromised by the (possibly electoral) agenda of local politicians. That agenda, it is argued, was rooted in an entrenched and overbearing local authority culture that insisted on trying to bend the programme for its own ends, simultaneously undermining its ability to properly address the needs of local people.

Territorialism and Active Citizens

Despite the NDC zone's clear outer boundaries, it could be divided into five or six sub-territories within those boundaries. These territorial divisions tended to be constructed informally by residents, or by housing tenure, or by 'natural' boundaries such as the main road or river. They were central to understanding the nature of social relations within the zone as a whole and contribute to how inhabitants of each territory experienced community, exclusion and related to the regeneration process. It was also a determinant of the nature and extent of community involvement. For example, at one of the residents meetings I attended, there were identifiably different agendas and concerns depending on the 'turf' one was on. One group, predominantly made up of residents who were owner-occupiers expressed anger at fly tipping.[4] Anger that seemed to be underpinned by an idea of 'deservingness' predicated on their status as homeowners: We pay good money for nice houses and live in a tip' (male resident and meeting attendee: 21–60). Moreover, this home owning status seemed to be used to legitimise claims on NDC and the local council. It also informed discussions about neighbourhood watch schemes (you get lower insurance) – an example of community engagement shaped by defending the 'respectability' of the estate.[5]

By contrast, another meeting, comprised predominantly of local authority tenants was dominated by worries about the threatened demolition of council housing. The residents in attendance discussed ways in which this could be avoided such as suggesting alternative housing management arrangements and vetting of potential tenants to root out 'troublesome' people or families who undermine the community fabric. Those who attended (therefore getting involved in the community) did so because of a threat to their property. It

---

4   The illegal dumping of refuse on unused or communal ground.

5   According to the NDC National Evaluation (CRESR 2003), in Salford homeowners accounted for 40 per cent of households in the NDC zone compared with 70 per cent across England. 40 per cent live in local authority housing within the zone compared to 20 per cent nationally.

seemed that different territories within the same NDC zone contained a different set of experiences and challenges for the inhabitants, which shaped, in turn, the way they do community and how their community should behave – either defensively to protect their interests, or assertively to challenge decisions. This also illustrated the heterogeneous reality of a community in which residents do not always share needs and interests and thus, the problem with making assumptions about their willingness to embrace the communal and unite beyond their own defined space.

In terms of a 'spirit' of community across the NDC zone as a whole (as opposed to within specific estates), there was some data to suggest that there was very limited interaction between territories and a lack of attachment to that overarching zone. For example, one female resident and community representative I interviewed began by stating how neighbourly and close knit her estate was, but went on to admit there was little contact with other local areas. The youth workers also spoke of this attitude amongst young people, where there was an almost tribal quality to their identification with certain local spaces or 'patch'. Their individual and group identities were partly constructed through the creation and maintenance of territorial boundaries. The spatial component of the construction and maintenance of youth identities may be obvious, but it does question the artificial construction of an NDC community and creates some problems in terms of the regeneration of that space. That is, if NDC imposed spatial boundaries that were incongruent with those already in existence, as constructed by local residents, there could be implications for attempts to successfully tackle exclusion and encourage residents to identify with and participate in local circuits of governance and decision making.

An interesting perspective on this issue was offered by students of the local university that I interviewed. None were from the area, but lived in halls of residence in the centre of the NDC zone. They identified, as illustrated by this exchange, not only their own sense of exclusion from everyday 'community' life, but a general lack of 'community' spirit amongst locals:

> C: We're not outsiders. I think we're just different aren't we. Two different groups of people – them outside the halls then there's us inside it really. That's what I mean, not having a local pub or owt, you wont get any community spirit between the two anyway … From just talking to people I know again it seems like there, I don't think they think there's much community spirit round here. I don't know why really, can't say, because you only talk about specific incidents when you do. Its either something really bad has happened or something really good but I don't know. The Prince of Wales [local pub] … I know people from round here who won't even drink in there. And that's the nearest pub to here... and even locals round here wont go in there so. Our cleaner, she's from Salford all her life and she says she won't go in any of pubs round here. I think that suggests what type of area it is.

Their dubiousness about local community spirit is rooted in a general feeling of unfriendliness, as expressed by the pub example. That is, if locals do not feel able to socialise there, that indicates a vulnerability based on a lack of trust. This point about factors that may illustrate a lack of, not just 'formal' engagement in civic life (such as volunteer work or community activity) but a lack of 'spirit' amongst local people, will be further explored in Chapter 6. Some examples were given in Chapter 4 of tensions between people, which undermined any aspirations or analysis of the space as a community inhabited by reflexive social agents with a sense of attachment to their locality and fellow residents – two factors upon which NDC's model of agency is founded.

'Good' Social Capital

Despite a lack of engagement in official NDC business, there was evidence of community involvement that could still be considered representative of the kind of civic engagement (and 'positive' agency) New Labour was keen to promote, what Mooney and Fyfe describe as 'good' social capital (2004: 19). Indeed, NDC introduced local 'Oscars' designed to reward community activity, even though that activity might occur out with official NDC channels. In the area, I encountered tenant and resident associations, parent toddler groups, lunch clubs for older people, a fruit and vegetable co-op and the Community Health Action Partnership (CHAP) which was set up by residents to organise and improve local health provision. Therefore, residents might not have been involved with official NDC mechanisms, but there were a variety of community groups and community businesses that indicated a desire on the part of some to form alliances and bonds with other residents as well as try to innovate service provision. In addition, there were informal support networks between local people, illustrating another brand of civic engagement. For example, the benefits of good neighbours was mentioned several times by residents such as an older man who expressed gratitude for having neighbours who will do things for him since he lives alone. Likewise, another older woman described her estate as 'very neighbourly', despite her neighbours' lack of interest in NDC specifically. Another example included a local woman:

AW: Ok. Would you say there was a sense of community?

C: Oh definitely, yeah. Everybody in my little area, we all look out for one another, watch our homes you know.

AW: What about beyond your immediate area, would you say? Say in Charlestown as a whole, is everyone on the same side or is there …

C: Oh I would say yeah, definitely. 'Cos we've all had the same problems. So you basically face the same things in your daily life don't you? ('Jane', resident: 21–60).

In her view, the problems of the area (beyond her street or estate) are coped with via a hardening of community bonds. Another resident proclaimed the strength of community feeling within his estate that had been harnessed to set up a residents association:

[Names estate] residents association. It would be good for you to come down and see what community support we've got. One thing you can say about this area is we have got good community, we all know each other and we've known each other for years so we can fall back on each other ('Jim', resident; 21–60: brackets added).

Tenants and residents associations were probably the clearest expression of this type of sentiment. At the last count, there were six across the NDC zone, each representing a distinct estate or area. The residents meetings I observed were reasonably well attended (21 at the first, 18 at the second and 13 at the third) although the first group were due to disband because no one would take over the chair from the woman standing down. There were also comments made at the third meeting about the unusually high turnout that month and the demolition plans seemed to have had a radicalising effect across the area generally, possibly distorting the normal levels of activity during my time in the field. These groups were relatively well attended, although they tended to be dominated by women highlighting a possible gender imbalance in 'community' involvement.[6] If so, this would reflect findings from other studies. For example:

Men described the sense of belonging they derived from participating in its various lodges, pubs and clubs, while women talked about the integrative potential and strength to be drawn from community networks. Community thus had a different meaning and was associated with different practices for men and women in coalmining regions (Parry 2005: 155).

Parry goes onto suggest that the sort of community work conducted by women may derive from their traditional role as informal care workers and that this relationship between care and community amounts to a 'local social organisation

---

6   A community worker confirmed this trend, arguing that community/voluntary groups tend to be dominated by women until they become 'big', then 'men arrive on the scene'. This may be a similar dynamic to that identified by Bea Campbell's (1993) study of urban unrest. In this case however it is an *engagement* with 'community' politics that is the context for an assertion of masculine power over women rather than the defiant or destructive rejection of local politics that Campbell found.

of labour' (2005: 161). The role of 'labour market positioning' (Parry 2005: 164) in influencing the extent and nature of residents' 'community' involvement was demonstrated in my study by the proportion of retirees involved in official NDC business. Furthermore, one male respondent mentioned how he had been made redundant and was officially unemployed. He implied his energies were concentrated at that time on organising community events and challenging various NDC initiatives. However, he spoke about how his assertive trade union training was not conducive to NDC's desire for consensual community:

> When I used to work, I used to work in an industry that was run by the unions, but I used to work in an environment which worked together with management and basically, my behaviour or me saying "that's not right" was looked upon as a good thing. I wasn't seen as a maverick ('Jim': 21–60).

Indeed, for many people, their immediate locality was their primary space and it was here that their key relationships were forged and where their social exclusion was experienced. Hence, the formation of such local services and networks, (many of which are organised on a voluntary basis) and a corresponding sense of community based around these services (a good example being the parent toddler group where users developed a bond around a shared experience of being a parent in the local area). However, involvement tended to be limited to specific groups, which have a narrow (possibly gendered, racialised) membership, such as older people's lunch clubs, or narrow agenda, such as housing issues. Interest in the wider community was bolstered by campaigns to block demolition plans, but in uneven ways, as we shall see in Chapter 6. Overall, residents seemed to experience multiple communities, with interests that occasionally overlapped. In addition, there were a range of contestations and conflicts that produced differential experiences of community and exclusion.

Radicalised Residents

One aspect of NDC that did have a radicalising effect on residents and engendered a greater sense of entitlement in terms of control over decisions affecting their neighbourhood was the demolition and redevelopment of housing. The empowerment rhetoric of NDC gave some residents a sense of legitimate opposition to what they viewed as complacent and self-serving local government and a rather untouchable regeneration process. There was an undoubted emboldening of some local residents with petitions organised, campaigns co-ordinated, officials challenged and banners hung around the affected estates. However, in spite of this spirited resistance, for some it was unfortunate that people only got community minded when opposing something – 'that people only get motivated when they are angry' ('Cath', resident: over 60). Nonetheless, NDC's presence did stimulate rather ad hoc examples of social capital and a sense of ownership. Not that NDC necessarily altered the consciousness of local people, but that the (perceived) contamination of the available community rhetoric of NDC by the development plans created conflict in which some sense of community and networks of social capital were stimulated and the supposed 'dependency culture' was indirectly challenged.[7] The tension between government – defined 'active' communities and those defined 'from below' has been explored in detail by Mooney and Fyfe. Using a case study of local resistance to the proposed closure of a swimming pool in Glasgow, they identify how local people formed networks of active social capital that the Scottish Executive 'would pay assorted consultants and community experts a small fortune to have achieved' (2004: 18). They go on to argue that New Labour distinguishes between 'good' social capital and 'bad' social capital and coming back to Salford NDC, it certainly appears that 'active' community is also a heavily circumscribed notion.

Many residents objected to the plans and took them as a sign of indifference or even active dislike towards local people:

> But the thing is, they never consulted us because they were buying this land with this plan anyway in mind cause the council know what they want to do. The council wants to turn this into like a Salford Quays, but they're not fucking people from round here. New Deal are meant to come here to look after us and alright bring new people into the area, but at the end of the day we [local residents] are the main thing about New Deal ('Jim', resident: 21–60, brackets added).

That is, for some local people, the 'development' framework was an attack upon the indigenous 'residents' and their sense of belonging and attachment to the estates that comprised the area. This was compounded by the sense that the regeneration (perhaps transformation is more apposite) of the area was being planned and implemented more or less in secret and that the local authority's enthusiasm for 'renewal' and change implied that local residents were somehow failing to sustain a 'strong', viable community.[8] The parallel that 'Jim' draws with the nearby Salford Quays development is interesting because the responses of residents

---

7   However, it is unclear whether we can translate this resistance into a challenge to paternalistic government per se. Paternalism or over-governing was not the major issue, more the perceived neglect of council estates and withdrawal of social housing.

8   Although the city council were suspected of using NDC to deliver the controversial plans to escape blame whilst also being able to brand it as 'regeneration'. Many were sceptical of the anti-exclusion benefits of such developments. For example, a community worker I interviewed voiced concerns about the redevelopment plans arguing that they amounted to a 'gentrification' of a poor, working class neighbourhood, legitimised on the basis that it 'doesn't pay for itself'. Another, a youth worker commented, 'New houses ... seems to be about regenerating an area rather than a community. The community is seen as an obstacle.'

have been reportedly similar to both. The NDC voluntary sector support worker – a Salfordian – argued that local people felt alienated by a huge development as Salford Quays feeling it was "not for them" and "not within their grasp". Some residents, illustrated by this exchange between two residents, also expressed this sense of exclusion from the local development plan:

Jim: [shouts to another female resident] What do you think of New Deal?

Female: Where's the money gone?

Jim: Thank you. Loads of fucking posh houses up there. [Points]

Female: Why can't we have them?

Jim: Oh no they're not for you! [sarcastic] You can't afford them, you're all the scrotes. Fuck off, you're getting nothing!

Jim: [aside] That's how they treat us at the end of the day, it's why we are the way we are ('Jim', resident: 21–60).

The tensions at the heart of regeneration programmes like NDC are laid bare by conflicts like these. The 'community' which is ostensibly at 'the heart' of the regeneration process functions both as a rationale and agent of local change, whilst also being the recipient of what Bourdieu (1991) termed 'symbolic violence' which maintains and reinforces the asymmetrical power relations between poor citizens and the state. NDC's attempts to transform the conditions of excluded neighbourhoods pivots around an implicit critique of the poor and their position relative to 'mainstream', 'socially included' society. By embodying and aspiring to a future of inclusion, renewal and prosperity through the marketing and restructuring of the local to attract new, wealthier residents, NDC conflates the past and present with stagnation, dependency and poverty – conditions which many local people either don't recognise, or if they do, feel were generated by processes of economic and political neglect and not by them. This was made worse by the model of agency underpinning NDC. In a sense, local 'active' citizens were valued as, and expected to be, agents of social change, but part of their 'new deal' was to buy into the implicit critique of their neighbourhood and 'culture' and drive the regeneration vision, thereby renouncing the moral and social conditions of their community and legitimising the mechanisms of social and physical change suggested by NDC. A significant challenge for NDC residents therefore was being engaged in the remaking of community by accepting the inferiority of the past and building a responsible, sustainable and profitable space where old habits are challenged and new ones forged. However, as shown with this example, this had repercussions in that many residents sensed, resented and challenged the dualism operationalised by NDC by objecting to what was considered an illegitimate takeover or 'urban snatch'. These residents felt let down by the local authority and had this compounded by a feeling of exclusion from the future trajectory of the neighbourhood. In the immortal words of one older female resident: 'we have had nothing for so long that we don't know what to ask for'. As a consequence some tried to disrupt rather than valorise the regenerative project and failed to perform their roles as transformative local agents. In light of this, I am not sure sufficient empathy and sensitivity was exhibited by NDC when engaging local citizens given the rather injurious aspects of this form of regeneration practice. There appears to have been a failure to recognise, or a disregard for the possibility of resistance to NDC plans and expectations. By promoting responsibility and the empowerment of local people, there was always the possibility of residents legitimately blocking initiatives and developments NDC deemed necessary or desirable for that area. As Atkinson notes,

> ... inscribed within the process of community participation are opportunities for resistance. Communities are not passive recipients of these initiatives, and although the balance of forces are weighted against them, there are possibilities to contest the ways in which initiatives are actualised at a local level within particular spaces; that is to pervert and bend the technologies of government in ways that the authors of particular programmes did not intend (2003: 106).

Conclusion

In Salford, NDC's relationship with the community it serves was a strained and often oppositional one. Beyond a few key community voices, there was very little involvement from local people and even that tended to be limited to participating in surveys, polls and questionnaires. NDC did perform an enabling role, with structures in place to facilitate community building through funding and advice for potential groups and network opportunities for existing groups within the NDC zone. However, probably NDC's biggest influence on community involvement and social capital was a rhetorical one. It was its rhetoric that sanctioned opposition to redevelopment plans for the area, and made for a situation in which residents and NDC managers were engaged in a struggle over the identity and future of the area. In an ironic twist, this struggle produced a scenario where the chief executive of NDC had to praise a residents group, via the NDC newsletter, who had successfully blocked NDC's own demolition plans.

Some of those who have engaged with the process did find it empowering just to feel some sense of involvement in the future of their neighbourhood:

> What has actually happened is that over the past three years, I've actually gained a lot of respect from all the councillors ... there are 5 councillors I could name ... and the local MP ... who are extremely supportive of me personally and that has actually come about through the New Deal process and through the activity that

I undertook within it. I think that part of that is recognising that the commitment that I have given but it is also about me learning more of the political game. Because you do have to play it. You just can't away with it. I hate it but you have to have it. I would say that over the past three years I've changed as a person … I know that I've grown substantially and I am not being immodest in saying that because I think it needs to be said because I think that it does recognise that the process can empower people ('Bill', resident and community representative: 21–60).

However, there were another strata of local people – those not involved or disinclined to get involved in the process – those residents who were largely just recipients of the NDC process, whose input was limited to voicing their opinions about the problems of their area (as demanded by surveys such as the PA consultation). Furthermore, there were other residents who actively sought to resist the 'renewal' of their neighbourhood. The example of housing redevelopment illustrates the messiness of the sites at which governance is produced and the negotiations and contestations that can infuse relations between citizens, the civic and the state, particularly when citizens appear to have been drawn into enactments of local government development strategy rather than as autonomous participants. In this case, the local state conveyed contradictory messages which sought to promote a local community sense predicated on shared identity, belonging and spatial proximity whilst implementing a physical development strategy that undermined and challenged that agenda. However, the ability or capacity of residents to inhabit this role and legitimise NDC in this way was undermined, not only by territorial difference, a sense of injustice or alienating channels of participation, but by the material and social exclusion they experienced. Chapter 6 will explore some of the dimensions of this exclusion and will discuss further the impact it had on the drawing in of residents to governance spaces like NDC.

Chapter 6
Making Sense of Social Exclusion

Introduction

My analysis of how NDC understood and sought to challenge the exclusion of neighbourhoods builds on the previous discussions of community and agency. It brings these together to argue how NDC's model of exclusion is predicated on problematic assumptions of unified experiences of poverty and disadvantage and a wellspring of active citizens participating in the governance space that NDC opened up. The chapter begins with a brief summary of how New Labour and NDC conceived of and tried and address social exclusion. Much of the critical analysis offered by this chapter is based on the critiques of community and agency from previous chapters, so here I draw on an important body of literature that builds on these and unsettles further how NDC sought to address the needs of local citizens. Finally, the chapter explores more data from my Salford case study that demonstrates the complexity of meeting the needs of a particular place via an area-based regeneration response.

New Labour, NDC and Exclusion

NDC was set up in 2001 to 'close the gap' between 39 of the most deprived neighbourhoods in England and the rest of society. This was structured around five key themes thought to underpin the exclusion of these neighbourhoods: poor individual health, poor quality housing, high levels of crime, educational underachievement and a rundown physical environment (Charlestown and Lower Kersal NDC Partnership 2009). Therefore, the model of social exclusion that New Labour propounded and NDC embodied contained three important dimensions. Firstly, individuals living in poverty experience structural disadvantages which negatively impact on their life chances. Secondly, this structural position can be exacerbated by inadequate local services and opportunities, such as poor schooling standards or a lack of public transport. That is, there is a direct link between 'area effects' and individual quality of life (Atkinson and Kintrea 2001: 2277). Thirdly, 'top-down' decision-making and service delivery can be disempowering and contribute to a sense of lack of control over one's life (Blears 2003: 22), hence the focus on community involvement and ownership.

Whilst NDC was designed to respond to rather than tackle the structural forces which produce excluded neighbourhoods, it did attempt to remedy the latter two contributors to exclusion. In terms of the second dimension, NDC appeared to operate on the basis that individual exclusion is a condition which is largely spatially determined and collectively experienced. That is, by virtue of living in an excluded space, residents of that space experience disadvantage in similar ways and have shared material needs. NDC's construction and mobilisation of community was a neat binding of the needs of individuals to the conditions of the neighbourhood tethering individual 'inclusion' to collective renewal. Therefore, the recognisability of these communities appeared to extend beyond an imputed sharing of identity and aspirations, into an assumed similarity of needs or problems. This then formed the basis of the solution – to identify the poor quality or gaps in service provision in an area and deliver resources to improve them. For the third dimension, NDC also sought to encourage residents to shape spending decisions and come up with innovative solutions to inadequacies in services, thus democratising service delivery and engendering a sense of ownership.

Diversity of the Welfare Subject

Whilst in a previous chapter I already discussed the diversity of community and problematised New Labour's understanding thereof, there is another important discussion of diversity that has taken place within recent debates about welfare policies. It seems appropriate to locate the discussion of NDC, a public welfare programme, not just in literature that emphasises community complexity, but also in broader debates about the division of welfare categories and its ability to respond to heterogeneity. This allows us to question the sophistication of both NDC's model of agency and social exclusion and invites us to consider what the implications might be for citizens drawn into local governance spaces without a adequate account of their individual structural position vis-à-vis economic and political systems and their relationships with other 'community members'.

Recent debates have sought to destabilise established or crude understandings of the welfare subject and instead, emphasise the diversity of welfare consumption patterns. There are two points that can be drawn out of this debate. On the one hand, there has been a growth in consumerist approaches to welfare in which users of services become diverse consumers who are empowered to exercise 'choice' of welfare packages and providers. A shift that can be framed – if we use Julian Le Grand's typology – to welfare users being considered empowered 'queens' rather than treated as passive 'pawns' (2003: 16). This conception of welfare subjects as individual consumers became a feature of New Labour governments and its desire to reform and 'modernise' public services (Jordan 2005; Clarke 2005). The centrality of 'choice' to New Labour's welfare agenda reflected their view of citizens as 'independent agents, rather than dependent subjects' (Clarke 2005: 449) and is concurrent with a Giddensian view of human agency that is 'self-actualised' – one that seeks to reflexively construct a personal biography through an array of 'lifestyle' choices, whether it be through selecting interpersonal relationships, ethical shopping or welfare packages.

Unsurprisingly, this agenda has received criticism, mainly for its neglect of the 'egalitarian and democratic spirit of membership' (Jordan 2005: 441) that public services such as the state education system and National Health Service in the UK are said to symbolise. That is, by stressing individual 'choice' as the framework for citizenship, there is a 'de-collectivising' of the public realm deemed intrinsic to social democratic governance (Clarke 2005: 449). On the other hand, sociological debate has approached this territory by stressing the need to reform welfare strategies to meet diverse needs, rather than consumer wants. This development of welfare responses is predicated on an attempt to develop an account of human agency that recognises,

> ... the dynamic between agency and structure needs to acknowledge the welfare subjects as creative agents, acting upon, negotiating and developing there own strategies of welfare management. They are not passive receivers of policy enactment, instead they help reconstitute the outcomes of and for informal policy provision (Williams and Popay 1999: 164).

As Deacon and Mann argue, it is vital to have greater recognition of agency within welfare debates, given the fragmentation of traditional categories of 'poor' and 'claimant'. They suggest:

> Work, family and the fixed identities of class, gender and community are more fluid ... The diverse constituencies that make up the poor will require more reflexive policies that attempt to support those who try to address their specific needs (1999: 431).

This was also the thrust of Williams, Popay and Oakley's call for a 'new paradigm' of welfare research that is: 'much more sensitive to the complex and dynamic structuring of people's health and welfare needs, their resources, their networks of support, their opportunities and their social relations' (1999: 5). However, as Ruth Lister commented, '(there has) been only limited engagement with attempts to forge a 'politics of difference' or 'recognition' ... issues of diversity and discrimination do not constitute central planks in the 'third way' (2000: 16). The point of briefly engaging with this debate is to problematise New Labour's understanding of excluded communities as largely unitary entities inhabited by agents with similar values, needs and aspirations by virtue of their shared community. This implies a lack of awareness of how welfare communities such as NDC areas actually contain a range of voices and experiences and how a collective of 'non-unitarist' selves may function. Therefore, the extent to which policy interventions such as NDC address the complexity of communities and the variety of needs they contain is a legitimate line of enquiry. It posits the question, from a welfare perspective, can an area-based programme like NDC adequately address the needs of a fragmented welfare constituency?

Understanding Exclusion

As with agency and community my research attempted to explore the model of exclusion that appeared to underpin NDC. That is, one that presumes that the needs of residents of an area can be identified and addressed on a geographical basis. In addition to examining the effectiveness and propriety of NDC's model of exclusion, I also wanted to develop an understanding of how social exclusion was experienced and lived by NDC residents; my hypothesis being that there were different experiences of social exclusion within a shared spatial context in keeping with the themes of complexity and contestation. In this section, the discussion is broken down into three parts, reflecting three ways in which individual resident's needs were configured. Firstly, the differential impact of a lack of service or facility is illustrated. That is, the fact that various social groups or individuals were affected by social exclusion in different ways depending on their age, disability, ethnicity and so on. Secondly, it is argued that within a defined geographical space there were a variety of needs that residents exhibited or articulated, some of which conflicted with those of other residents. The final part is an exploration of how needs are shaped relationally, in contact with other residents' attitudes and behaviour. The key point here being that how excluded people relate to each other – how individuals 'get on' is a fundamental aspect of how exclusion is experienced. Some of the data here overlaps with that used to illustrate how community is contested; the difference here is the analytical objective. In this case, the purpose is to illustrate some of the effects of these processes of contestation on the quality of lives of residents. Not only is contestation an interesting process in itself for its implications for theorising community, but it has analytical value in developing understandings of the experiencing of social exclusion. For example, contestations of space, such as the conflict around children's play areas become not just illustrations of 'contested community', but have a direct impact upon the quality of life for some young people because they are actively deprived of a play area. Moreover, other (older) residents are excluding young residents from a stake in the renewal discourse of NDC by arbitrating (and rejecting) their claims. Similarly, negative feelings towards asylum seekers can be viewed both as an example of a process indicative of a stratified neighbourhood, as well as having real effects for how asylum seekers experience their exclusion if those 'negative feelings' turn nasty. Therefore, this chapter, is about the translating some of the same data around contestation into a discussion of the diversity of social exclusion.

Differential Impact of Exclusion

Understanding and tackling exclusion is about understanding the needs of individuals and how those needs are shaped. In terms of excluded NDC residents, I want to argue that a key part of the configuration of need is the interaction of local residents with poor local services. The occurrence of a 'differential' impact emphasises, as a starting point, the inadequacy of local services as a key driver of social exclusion, then considers how different social groups are affected by that inadequacy. It is not sufficient to simply state, for example, that residents were socially excluded because bus services were poor in this NDC zone. For a better understanding of excluded experience, one must reflect upon the lives of local residents themselves. How does the poor bus service impact upon people's lives – presumably not uniformly, but in more subtle and varied ways. If so, how does this configure needs and what are the implications for residents?

The scope of local needs was illustrated, in this study, around a few key issues in the neighbourhood. That is, as one would expect in a space containing a range of social groups, a range of needs were exhibited. For example, to return to the public transport example, older people who were interviewed spoke often about the poor quality of public transport – something which they relied on a great deal for shopping, visiting friends and family and attending hospital appointments. Public transport was an issue for several residents across the board, including some young people wanting quick, cheap access to shopping districts; however, the isolation engendered by a poor bus service appeared to be made more acute by the lack of physical mobility and financial resources experienced by many older people. For example, one older man noted that there was only one bus per hour in his area since services were cut "due to vandalism". Another mentioned how he gets a taxi to the local shopping precinct due to poor bus service, 'We pay council tax for decent buses, but don't get the service. I think they have forgotten we exist down here' (male resident: over 60). This need for better public transport links (meaning buses, since the local train station had been closed and the tram network did not extend into the area), seemed to be exacerbated by the lack of adequate shopping facilities nearby. Within the NDC zone, there were few shops offering only a limited choice of provisions. These shops were found on the main thoroughfares, a relatively long distance from some of the outer estates of the zone. Again, an issue for all residents, but especially pronounced for those residents without cars or with physical mobility problems. For example, one older female reported that her area within the zone was very isolated with poor bus service and no shops. She prioritised above all else more basic shops such as grocery stores and newsagents to prevent older people having to walk too far – at that time the only 'service' in her immediate area was a rather unprepossessing local pub.

By contrast, young people interviewed articulated shopping needs in keeping with their own social milieu. Suggestions for the neighbourhood included fast food restaurants with take away facilities, sportswear and other clothes shops as well as a tanning salon. They were less concerned with any perceived lack of good grocery shops, preferring to prioritise fashion and leisure related outlets. Therefore, the perceived absence of different services or facilities from the local area (helping define an area as excluded) produced varying experiences of that absence and consequently, varying responses/needs, depending upon the circumstances of the resident. One caveat being that age is only one indicator when discussing need. Of course, some older people will be able to use existing shops or be able to afford cars. Similarly, there will be some young people who 'need' more grocery shops.

Another example was the lack of adequate leisure facilities in the NDC zone. Most young people identified this as something 'missing' from their community. That is, the social exclusion of young residents was less defined by inadequate local shops and more about having 'nothing to do' with their leisure time. Again, the absence of regular public transport exacerbated this problem, making it difficult for young people to travel to other facilities.[1] This need was expressed through suggestions for a new skate park, sports centre, gymnasium, motorbike track and youth or recreation centre. Just 'somewhere for us to go' was the response of one young male. Another was, '[we need] more things for teenagers to do, because of boredom' (Female resident, under 21, brackets added). One teenage male, residing in a local hostel for homeless young people confirmed there was 'nothing to do ... there is fuck all in the area.'

For many young people, the absence of legitimate 'private' space (outside the home) provided by such facilities led them to occupy 'public' spaces within the NDC zone. Therefore, certain shops or bus shelters were colonised by relatively large groups of young people in the evening. Football was played in a pub car park or on the bowling green whilst the playing fields were used for barbeques and generally 'hanging about'. Male youths on motorbikes rode around the estates or on the playing fields, lacking as they did a legitimate place, sanctioned by the community, to pursue their interest. As shown in the previous section on contested spaces, this occupation of public space could produce conflict with adult residents. The local police sergeant expressed this issue thus:

> Erm, there is a lot of frustration. The kids don't want to stay in obviously they want to be out and they're frustrated because they don't want to be on the streets seen to be intimidating, but they're bored they've nowhere to go, erm, and if anyone has a go at 'em – they retaliate, causing damage ...

Often this was interpreted as 'antisocial' behaviour by adult residents. There were also references made in interviews about the 'unruliness' of young people and a perceived lack of respect for authority.

A further complexity is the way in which older people responded to this occupation of public space. The PA survey found feelings of intimidation concerning youth gangs around shops. One older female resident supported this finding:

---

1 However, there was a definite sense of locality when speaking to residents – an expectation that *this* area should provide leisure services. Instead of attributing this to an instinctive sense of community, as NDC appeared to do, I would suggest it had more to do with residents tacitly complying with the way the area has been isolated, driven by cuts in bus services, closure of the local train station and an allegedly ambivalent local authority.

Erm, there is a shop down on the other side of Gerald Road, I wouldn't go in there late at night to save me life ... and they're all in there sat on fridges and all sorts, it's very, very intimidating ('Jane', resident: 21–60).

The local sergeant corroborated this sentiment:

[Fear] ... of the noise on the streets, the intimidating youths gathering. People don't want to use the shops, they don't want to come out because of the noise – so it's a fear, erm, more than anything really which is unfortunate (brackets added).

Certainly, on the evenings I was in the area, it was usual to see groups of young people congregating around shops, some trying (often successfully) to purchase alcohol. Therefore, the presence of young people in public could affect how older people experience the neighbourhood and added another dimension to their exclusion. For example, the PA survey found that 'elderly' people adopted strategies to avoid this 'threat', not leaving home after a certain time and making sure they did any shopping in the morning. Not only do some older people suffer from the lack of shopping facilities, they could also feel intimidated when using the shops that do exist.

However, older people were not the only group 'threatened' by the presence of young people on the streets:

I class myself as someone who isn't usually bothered by a few yobs down street alley but I think things are getting worse like kids chucking clumps of rock at you. Like I was walking down [names street], it was only a couple of week ago and we were coming back and they were chucking great big blocks of concrete at you. If I feel a bit unsure walking home on a night I can only imagine what a lot of other people feel like ('Colin', student: under 21).

Some adult residents recognised the need for more facilities for young people, usually rooted in eradicating the threat and 'nuisance' they create, rather than challenging their exclusion. For example,

Give them somewhere like say a café type. Where they just sold soft drinks and cups of tea and things like that. Somewhere they could go and sit, with their friends, their mates, whatever, if the weather was bad you know? ... It would take them off the street corners. Ok, so they're all in one congregated area but they're not causing the neighbours any problems are they? [if they're in a café] They're not getting up to mischief they get up to now ... they're just bored. Nothing else to do. So they'll go and do somebody's car in or pinch somebody's car ('Jane', resident: 21–60, brackets added).

However, as discussed above, the blocking of youth shelters by adult residents suggests this was going to be difficult to implement successfully. Moreover, the planned and recent leisure developments were criticised by local youth workers who doubted the inclusionary credentials of such projects. For example, on the new football-specialist sports village: 'It's taking the piss. First of all you have to like football, then because it's a centre of excellence, you have to be good at it! How is that inclusionary? ('Paul' youth worker). Similarly, the recently opened Astroturf pitch next to the new school is only open to the youth service and local groups if they pay a rental fee ('how is that inclusion?').

Young people did seem to suffer disproportionately from inadequate leisure facilities in the area due, mainly, to their need for interaction with peers and 'something to do' with their free time. This manifested itself in a reliance on public spaces as a resource for leisure pursuits and often resulted in conflict with adult residents. Increased policing of these spaces (new CCTV cameras could be found on main roads and around shopping areas) and greater scrutiny of behavioural standards (is it antisocial?) by local police and some residents all combined to produce an experience of exclusion that differed from other members of the 'community' and configured a distinctive 'need' – rooted in being a certain age. Of course, all residents could have potentially benefited from a new sports centre for example, but no other groups were so dependent on spaces outside the home for socialising but were so un-catered for whilst being subject to so much scrutiny.

Specific Needs

Other configurations of need were identified that were not about differential impacts of 'poor' services, but originating in the specific experiences of certain groups and individuals. An example might be the suggestion, made by a carer for disabled people, to lower the kerbs in the area, particularly on the road leading to the local cemetery to make visits easier. She made the point that for wheelchair users, having to negotiate high kerbs when going anywhere around the local area made the journey very uncomfortable. It is unlikely that any other group in the area would have made this suggestion, but it was a need for this group, rooted in their individual experience. Furthermore, another priority was more jobs suitable for disabled people: 'There are lots of people in here who are capable of carrying out tasks but its finding an outlet where they can perform these tasks' ('Jane', resident and carer: 21–60). Indeed, job opportunities were mentioned by several residents, some in relation to working for NDC itself, and others in a general sense – notably some young male respondents. However, according to the 2004 NDC Delivery Plan, 90 per cent of local businesses rated the NDC area as 'poor' in terms of the skills and employability of local people. NDC was trying to remedy this apparent mismatch between opportunities and skills by publicising the local 'job shop' and had a programme in development rather ominously entitled 'Maximising Local Labour', designed to 'assist people into the construction industry' (Charlestown and Lower Kersal NDC Partnership (2004: 14). Whether such a scheme met the employment needs is unclear given the advent of recession, but the tagline did raise fears similar to those expressed with regard to the government's New Deal workfare programme (see Levitas 1998).

New types of housing were also identified as an important need of some disabled people:

> There are an awful lot of people who would love to live independently but can't because of the housing, because of the structure of certain houses, because there are very, very few bungalows in this area ('Jane', resident and carer: 21–60).

Another example of a specific need was for older people in the area. One interviewee, the NDC partnership chair, made the point that older people require more proactive engagement to ensure their needs are met:

> We've got a growing older population, after the baby boom, after the war and I don't think we're addressing their needs, because the presumption is that when you get to 60, retirement age for a lady, you'll want to go and sit in the day centre round the corner. Most people, now the life expectancy has moved on, want more than that.

This could apply to a range of needs including more leisure opportunities, continued job opportunities in retirement age or more opportunities for involvement in the local community and voluntary sector.

Other specific needs identified included more community support for informal carers in the area; more support for those experiencing manageable health problems; alley gating for some houses to block motorbike runs (eventually completed on some estates) and concerns about high asthma rates and chest related problems in a housing estate that bordered a heavy industrial estate. A support worker who noted that local hostels do not meet the basic standards of cleanliness or heating identified better accommodation for asylum seekers as the key need of that group. The support worker also thought that the accommodation of certain groups in unsuitable housing displayed a lack of cultural sensitivity.

These were just some of the examples given of specific needs, related to specific groups living in the NDC neighbourhood. They give a flavour of how within a relatively small space, a range of distinct needs can be found and emphasise the importance of consulting all groups to ascertain the variety of needs and developing subtle responses. However, difficulties can arise if one need clashes with another or the concerns of another. The youth shelters being a good example of the tension that can sometimes obscure the specific need that was exhibited in the first place.

Social Relations and the Mediation of Need

Individual need as a response to conditions of social exclusion is not just about how lives can be improved through new or better services. The way needs are configured can also be related to experiences of social relations as discussed at length in Chapter 4. That is, the way community and exclusion are lived is usually through the prism of human relationships. This grass root, relational reality can have a bearing on the needs that agents exhibit and how successful regenerative projects are when trying to address apparently 'straightforward' indicators of 'exclusion'. For example, the reality of living in the NDC zone for many young people was one where territorialism provided a sense of identity in addition to spatial boundaries for 'hanging around'. This point was first made by local youth workers who described a situation where youths from either sides of the river that bisected the zone did not mix socially. This had implications for their development work, forcing them to allocate time to several different territories over the course of the week. Some young people interviewed confirmed this territorial pattern; a pattern apparently shaped by fear of certain places and people. For example, one teenage male stated that he avoided specific estates due to "big gangs of lads". Two other younger males also told of how they avoided certain places for fear of having their bikes stolen by local gangs and how they never ventured across the river. Even within one area of the zone, there were three distinct territories and associated identities: 'uptowners', 'midtowners' and 'downtowners', all inhabiting an estate no larger than a square mile. The informal way in which these identities were constructed was illustrated to me by an encounter with a group of 'uptowners'. The youth worker whom I was accompanying was eager to convince the group of young males to appear in the local newspaper alongside a mural they had designed for a local wall to publicise what she argued was a positive expression of youth identity. The lads, however, were extremely resistant to the idea, fearing it would make them look 'gay' and like 'goons'. The formalising of their identity in the media would (it appeared) have engendered an immediate loss of status and undermined the informal, organic nature of their territorial identity not to mention their esteem in the eyes of rival groups.

This data around territorialism can been used to de-stabilise the notion of a 'recognisable' spatial community upon which NDC is predicated (a notion that also underpinned how need is constructed and addressed within that space). The data shows that within the zone, young people formulated their own communities, often based around a very small geographical areas. Thus, there was little interaction between these sub-groups of youths and when there was, it appeared to manifest in conflict or around transcendent spectacles such as police chases or joy riders such as the incident with the caravan recounted in Chapter 4. Moreover, in terms of configuring needs, this territorial reality had an impact because it shapes how young people experienced their exclusion in this area – in a bounded geographical space. How effective is it therefore, to build new facilities in one specific area of the NDC zone? According to one youth worker, new projects such as the youth centre that was under construction 'will be great'. However, he made the point that whilst in theory all local young people could use it, territorialism may prevent some from accessing this resource because it is not on 'their patch'. Another example came from the youth service itself. Their base was to the south of the river whereas one set of young females they worked with lived to the north. They were in the process of trying to coax them across the river to the service base to conduct some indoor work, but without success. This was constructed as a 'test' to force the girls to 'prove' their commitment to the youth workers in return for more funding applications on their behalf. They were not forthcoming at the time however, because it was 'across the river and not their patch' (female youth worker). The girls' access to support and opportunities via the youth workers was being diminished by their territorial attachment and fear of other estates. Therefore, the configuration of young people's needs was shaped, to an extent, by social relations 'on the ground', determined largely, by territorial division. This is an illustration of how people themselves can organise and stratify the excluded neighbourhood in informal ways. Consequently, tackling exclusion and addressing need is not as straightforward as identifying something that is missing from the area, remedying the context and thereby improving the lives of that group. That 'remedying' takes place within a relational context that must be recognised and understood for its potential impact.

Another example of this relational dimension to experiencing exclusion came from the data generated around the experiences of asylum seekers in the area. Whereas young people could at least construct their own territorial identity, asylum seekers had much less scope for formulating such modes of resistance. Their status as 'space invaders' meant that at the time I was conducting fieldwork they were usually victims of 'othering' by 'indigenous' residents sometimes manifesting in overt violence and aggression. Data to illustrate the 'othering' process was recounted in Chapter 4 and there was some evidence that the relational level through which asylum seekers experienced exclusion included incidents of violence and abuse. One resident and chair of the partnership board put it to me that, '... the vast majority of the community take these people very much as part of their community once they come and live with us. I don't think there is much animosity towards people.' However, by contrast, several other examples were given to me of violence and abuse towards this group. Whether that was the story of the attack on accommodation centres where asylum seekers were housed as documented in Chapter 4, or the Kurdish family who had their front windows smashed and, according to the refugee support worker I interviewed, had a petrol bomb thrown through their window. Similarly, a local youth worker claimed a Yemeni family had to take refuge in a local mosque after the father was 'battered by local lads'. Overall, the support worker alleged that there is a 'great deal of violence' towards asylum seekers and 'verbal abuse is common' because they are an 'easy target'. She also claimed four families with whom she was working who have had 'cars stolen, burnt out or windows smashed'. This reflects a finding of Dwyer and Brown's study of refugees and their experiences of leaving reception centres and moving into 'communities' where they can be subjected to harassment and violence at the hands of neighbours (2005: 375). In Salford, local media had recently reported the serious assault of a young Kurdish male and a Latvian male in an area bordering the NDC zone.

It could be argued that asylum seekers and refugees experienced a disproportionate amount of violence and conflict than other groups within and around the NDC zone, with the exception perhaps of young people. Their social exclusion was one compounded by often hostile or intolerant social relations within the area, which configured their 'needs' beyond the material to encompass an experiential reality that is shaped by social agents and fellow residents.

One of the original intentions of this research was to explore the tendency on the part of policymakers to conceptualise exclusion as a spatially (and thereby materially) determined condition. In addition, whilst not denying the structural/institutional dynamics that produce such excluded spaces, to contrast this with an analysis of internal dynamics within such spaces (NDC communities) and how exclusion is experienced in different ways, manifesting in a variety of needs and shaped by internal social relations with other residents. As we have seen, primarily, this heterogeneity centres on the way in which the absence of certain services has a differential impact on people according to their different social locations. That is, residents do not experience exclusion uniformly (if exclusion is exemplified by an absence of something within a certain space, such as inadequate public transport provision). The way in which it is lived is shaped by age, locality, gender, ethnicity, disability, socioeconomic status and so on. This produces a 'community' of welfare recipients who have differing needs and varying responses to their excluded condition. In addition, this may have implications for the effectiveness of regeneration attempts if there is a failure to appreciate this lack of uniformity and recognise both the quantity of needs alongside the qualitative configuration of those needs, particularly where they appear to challenge the consensual model of community that underpins NDC. The exclusion of some groups is actually constituted and shaped by their membership of a spatially bounded community. I would argue, the consequence is a stratified policy terrain patterned by shifting excluded social and economic positions requiring subtle welfare responses rather than a unitary, stagnating excluded community awaiting a 'surgical strike' (Furbey 1999: 433) of regeneration.

Conclusion

This chapter concludes my analysis of the three concepts of community, agency and exclusion deemed here to underpin NDC. In summary, my critique of NDC is that it represented an example of a governance space and a mechanism of regeneration that drew local residents into circuits of decision-making and absorbed them into new social and political formations. The reinvigorated communities which NDC sought to build and strengthen were normative socio-political products to which residents were expected to submit and propel. However, this process of regeneration was predicated on some flawed assumptions about the life of poor neighbourhoods and the people that inhabit such spaces. I would argue that they are sites which are socially excluded in a structural sense, but which are mediated through sets of social relations producing a contested, fractured and heterogeneous terrain. These are important discussions in themselves and in these chapters I have sought to argue for more nuanced accounts of the social within spatially bounded, disadvantaged spaces. This has led me towards accounts of community, agency and exclusion which identify the contingent, interlocking complexities of each, facilitating an analysis of NDC models as somewhat anaemic constructs. However, I want to move beyond these discussions now and explore the implications for residents of being drawn into governance spaces on the basis of these constructed local citizenships and how this experience impacts upon the potential for greater autonomy and justice. In my penultimate chapter, I will frame my discussions in political terms to understand why NDC neighbourhoods and their residents have been conceived in such an apparently flawed manner (that is, why did localised welfare governance develop like this under New Labour), and examine what this meant for their 'inclusion' and 'empowerment'.

Chapter 7

Ensnared Citizens

Introduction

The previous three chapters have extensively problematised what we might consider the rationality of the NDC programme, embodied in the models of community, agency and exclusion. My critical starting point was that this rationality failed to deliver for many residents in NDC spaces because it functioned to obscure the complexities that shape everyday poverty experience. This meant that NDC and its assumptions complicated and inhibited the new governance spaces that residents found themselves negotiating. Furthermore, these were spaces which generated pressures on residents to participate effectively since occurring alongside and framing the NDC rationality for regenerating poor spaces was an attempt by the central state to draw in spatial territories and their inhabitants as co-producers of institutional, social and cultural change. This can be understood as an example of policy decision-making and implementation being rescaled to sub-national levels to reform or 'modernise' governing practice and reinvigorate civic space as a locus of policy innovation, collective expression and cultural meaning (Wallace 2009). NDC was an innovative intervention, enacting a wider impulse constituting residents as active policy actors and communities as 'total place' policy arenas (DCLG 2010) in which multiple local challenges could be addressed, whilst also regenerating the interior living spaces and culture of the urban poor making neighbourhoods secure, liveable and sustainable. The bolstering of individual and collective agency was said to enhance the self-governance of subaltern neighbourhoods deemed to have been failed in the past by 'parachuted' state interventions, rewarding those who wanted to exercise greater local control whilst, in a more normative vein, responsibilising local citizens in order to valorise the strong, inclusive communities of New Labour's communitarian imagination. NDC reflected an attempt to transform 'striated' places' into 'smooth', governable 'spaces' (see Osbourne and Rose 2004; Taylor 1999).

However, there are clearly important questions to be asked about the 'turn to the local' in welfare policy arrangements (Wallace 2009) and how it interlocks with the rationality of NDC. Situating my analysis of NDC within debates about the form and motivation of contemporary welfare governance, this chapter engages in discussions about New Labour's rhetorical commitment to the empowerment of citizens, inviting us to consider how we make sense of a political project that intensified the discourse of active, inclusive citizenship whilst apparently failing to take account of how citizenship capability is produced and lived. NDC neighbourhoods were ideal spaces in which to explore this tension. This chapter also attempts to draw together some of the threads of my analysis thus far to make sense of the implications of the disconnection between the community and exclusion experience mapped out in these chapters and the assumptive communities and citizenships inherent in New Labour's recipe for the urban poor. That is, not only do we need to think critically about the NDC as a space of governance from the point of view of 'empowering' welfare shifts, but also as an attempt to understand, shift and harness the agency of the poorest citizens. What was the balance of citizenships here and what were the implications for enhanced autonomy and social justice?

Disconnected Communities

The key theme of this discussion is disconnection. Not only in terms of the identification of excluded, subaltern spaces deemed 'excluded' and apart from mainstream society and in need of policy intervention, or in terms of the 'deficit' between citizens and state thought to undermine democratic systems and compound poverty and disadvantage, but the disconnection that underpins the welfare responses to these two key problematics of modern governance. If this book has tried to do anything, it has attempted to illustrate the binary distance that exists between New Labour's evaluative and normative take on poor communities and the actual, politicised realities of these entities. A useful way of thinking about this disparity has been to consider 'community' as a product. New Labour envisaged communities as socio-spatial resident-products behaving in predictable, consensual ways, willing and able to participate in assemblages of governance. This was predicated on residents identifying and engaging with a spatially-bounded territory and imbuing it with sufficient meaning to want to enact particular moral and behavioural codes in order to create, strengthen and defend the integrity of their local-social. In contrast, I have argued that community can indeed be considered a product, but one that is not fixed at any point in time or place. Moreover, it is a product of social agents who have varying needs, values and experiences combining to generate unstable sites of social, economic, political and cultural exchange. The tension between these conflicting understandings of community and local citizenship generates a number of important questions. Thus far, the book has tended to focus on the effect of this disconnection on residents' capacity to address the poverty of their neighbourhood and interact with the regeneration experience. However, the present discussion will explore reasons why this gap exists, bringing in some critical literature to examine possible broader explanations.

Firstly however, another important layer of analysis must be added here and that is to suggest that gaps or disconnections that exist between government prescriptions and local realities can of course be considered one of the vicissitudes of policy implementation. If we take Salford NDC area as an example, it is tempting to ask, in light of the complexities and territorial divisions, how it was selected for

NDC funding in the first place. If there were criteria of cohesion and consensus to be met, surely this area will have struggled to convince budget holders and policymakers.

It is worth pausing to consider how this was interpreted on the ground. For some respondents, the answer was that the selection of this area had little to do with its strong identity or consensual fabric, but was a politically motivated decision. For example, there was an impression on the part of one NDC staff member in Salford that this area was given the money not because of the community spirit of the area, but because it was simply 'their turn'. That is, that other wards in the city were receiving funding from other regeneration streams (such as Single Regeneration Budget) and these estates had fallen behind in the pursuit of government resources. Consequently, NDC funding was targeted to plug a gap in the Salford-wide neighbourhood renewal strategy. Furthermore, a resident respondent suggested that the choice of these areas (out of all wards across Salford as a whole) as the 'bid' wards for NDC funding within this strategy was down to political expediency and the desire to boost the profile and popularity of local politicians. Another mooted explanation for its selection was the perceived 'potential' of the area given the amount of unused land and access to the valuable riverside. This was certainly the impression of some of the more conspiratorial residents who believed the NDC process had been a Trojan horse for the local authority eager to sell off this dormant land for development purposes and alter the social mix of an area that 'doesn't pay for itself' ('Karen': community worker).[1] Overall, understanding why this area was explicitly chosen is difficult to discern with any certainty. There appears to be two factors. On the one hand, there was some definite local shaping in terms of delineating this particular zone in preparation for bidding, possibly under political influence. Added to this is the role of the architects of the initial NDC bid in Salford who would have worked within two strategic planning frameworks. The first would have been the Local Strategic Partnership's neighbourhood renewal strategy. The NDC bid would have had to compliment this locally constructed area development framework and the city council's vision for the city as a whole. The second was the central government guidelines as supplied by the Neighbourhood Renewal Unit. For example:

> Charlestown and Lower Kersal was identified as the preferred area for New Deal for Communities by the Salford Partnership, the strategic partnership for the City ... The neighbourhood stands out as an area of Salford which exhibits concentrated problems ... These problems accord with the priority issues that 'New Deal for Communities' has been established to tackle (Charlestown and Lower Kersal NDC Delivery Plan 2001a: 5).

---

1   Certainly, the re-branding of Salford as a whole has been related to the redevelopment of the river that runs through it. An article in a local newspaper (Keeling 2005) reported how consultants had identified the riverbank as a resource that if successfully regenerated could attract people to live and work there.

Consequently, the initial NDC bid sought to portray the area as containing potential for development, being relatively homogeneous and crucially, consensual. For example,

> Despite the area's decline, Charlestown/Lower Kersal has a well defined community with strong links across the area in terms of family, services, jobs, education and community perceptions (Charlestown and Lower Kersal NDC Partnership Delivery Plan 2001: 5).

Therefore, responsibility for allowing this space to be considered a recognisable community and the consequent disconnection between image and reality lay partly with the architects of the bid in Salford, not just civil servants in Whitehall. Despite the complexity of local community, they were able to portray the area as required by central government guidelines whilst meeting their own local strategic social and planning needs. The demands of government funding requirements seemed to have necessitated a (re)constitution of this space, by local planners, as a consensual community, based on a rather partial analysis, simultaneously obfuscating the complex reality of relationships in the area.

Nonetheless, whilst one can understand the desire (or belief) on the part of local people and planners to attract NDC funding and so portraying their area in the manner which is demanded, this is a layer of analysis that is somewhat besides the substantive point under discussion here which is to examine why a flawed rationale of community was used to underpin NDC policy directives. The essence of this question is, in the course of enacting problematic constructs of community and agency, were policymakers aware of this detachment? Also, were they aware of the problems this may present for NDC partnerships on the ground that had to manage the tensions and conflicts that their programmes were supposed to avoid (by virtue of only being awarded to 'recognisable communities'?). In short, was NDC a deliberate strategy to deliver short-term local gains and distract attention from a lack of action on wider structures of inequality and in so doing disregarding the challenges of understanding the local, or was it an attempt to regulate excluded citizens and problem estates by enacting specific expressions of community, thereby deepening state-driven norms of behaviour.

Management, Control or Neglect?

Key questions for any welfare programme that seeks explicitly to empower and socially include citizens are going to be the degree of authenticity of those objectives and how to measure their success. In light of successive urban policy failures and the suspicion that governments are only ever concerned with more effective means of citizen control, the common critical response is to ask whether individuals have the power to set and challenge agendas, decide priorities and allocate resources, or are they merely incorporated into established methods of governance and decision-making? If the latter is the case, then even if a given programme was successful in 'empowering' the majority on these terms, logic follows that this would have little bearing on their socially excluded status; it would simply mean a legitimising of the status quo. NDC's eagerness to 'animate' local residents and put 'communities at its heart' raised suspicions about the role of participation and empowerment as part of an overall strategy to 'socially include'. In light of the evidence presented in earlier chapters, it is clear that NDC – at least in Salford – failed to engage and empower many residents in a meaningful way. Some explanations for the disconnection noted here have been suggested throughout the book, with attention paid to the difficulty of transforming complex 'places' into governable 'invited spaces' (see Taylor 1999), a failure to appreciate locally ingrained mistrust of government agencies and impinging political and economic forces on the shape and behaviour of the NDC regeneration approach in Salford. All of these militated against well-grounded, developmental processes that could have enhanced the regeneration experience for many local people. However, in light of some of the themes generated by the response of residents in Salford combined with some pertinent critical literature around regeneration and new governance spaces, I want to widen my analytical scope to try and unsettle the NDC programme further in order to propose further explanations for the aforementioned failures.

Firstly, there is the 'sticking plaster' argument; that NDC amounted to little more than a *managerial* response replete with governance practices that were actually containment strategies for the poor. This is as opposed to concentrating on reforming the wider inequalities that create excluded spaces, or empowering citizens so that they can challenge wider structures themselves. As such, Amin suggests that community was a key rationality in the 'repackaging of the economy and society' associated with the Third Way (Amin 2005: 614) and a means of segregating and localising the socioeconomic problems generated by neo-liberalism. This resulted in the construction of 'excluded' interstitial communities as objects of policies encouraging self-governance and renewal but decoupled from wider, more profound economic or political strategies. Amin notes: 'the local has been re-imagined as the cause, consequence, and remedy of social and spatial inequality' (Amin 2005: 614). Notwithstanding the 'victim blaming' possibilities of this approach, the key issue here is that it hardly matters therefore that NDC failed to properly account for the politicised dynamics of community or the deleterious impacts of poverty and failed citizen-state relations on participative citizenship, since the goal was to deliver extra resources to poor estates, whilst binding residents to localised struggles concerned with re-ordering dysfunctional communities as self-regulating entities. This has been a common criticism of the community empowerment rhetoric that New Labour embraced and links with a broader critique of New Labour's perceived ignoring of the structural determinants of poverty in favour of welfare activation (see Alcock 2004; Levitas 1998). Indeed, in this sense, NDC becomes analogous with Giddens' 'autotelic self' in that it is seen to be a pragmatic measure that accepts the context of power in which it operates and concentrates on 'renewal' through re-branding and building 'capital'. NDC is then designed to create 'autotelic' communities of residents that can cope with the post-traditional risks and uncertainties not of their making. The 'empowerment' and 'participation' of local citizens can then allow for the retrenchment of the role of the state in public welfare systems. However, as Alcock (2004) has warned, the fashion for citizen participation could have gone too far in the opposite direction with a drift towards bottom-up policy planning being in danger of pathologising the problems of poor neighbourhoods which are generated by wider structural dynamics. Lupton agrees: 'ultimately, we will not bring an end to the problems of 'Poverty Street' ... unless we are also prepared to challenge seriously the inequalities in our economy and our society that are the real causes of relative poverty and of social exclusion' (2003: 220). Similarly, for some, programmes such as NDC should be complimented by action on the wider causes of exclusion, not just the local level: 'the success of neighbourhood regeneration programmes depends on wider action to address regional economic divisions' (Lister 2001: 432). Benington and Donnison have voiced similar concerns: 'a small area focus of this kind can run the risk of diverting attention away from the wider political economic forces which cause and maintain the concentrations of poverty and unemployment in these areas' (1999: 65). This was a critical theme picked up on by one of my respondents ('Carol', community worker) who characterised the NDC as a 'sticking plaster' for a deeper problem and questioned whether it was tackling the 'root causes of exclusion.' According to this logic, the techniques of 'empowering' residents and 'building community' are about the avoidance of radical change by seeking to change local behaviour to be more responsible and less passive and possibly (social) welfare dependent, rather than addressing the regional, national or global structures that create and perpetuate neighbourhoods in poverty. Judged against this criterion it is hard to argue that NDC offers much in terms of egalitarian, anti-poverty objectives and it casts its participation agenda in a rather pale light, particularly for those tasked – like 'Carol' – with affecting change in those neighbourhoods. However, whilst this form of analysis does provide a valid perspective on how local projects operate within wider constraints, I think we need to think a bit more subtly when analysing programmes like NDC and how they impinge on the possibilities of local citizenship. The drawing in of local people to projects of regeneration and governance presents a range of connected issues which go beyond the undoubted limitations of local area initiatives. The more pertinent of these for this discussion relates to the contours of this new community governance role and the political dynamics that have driven this shift to dispersed sites of governance. Certainly, it is tempting to characterise NDC as being designed to manage problem spaces and somehow distract attention from New Labour's unwillingness to perform radical surgery on the economic structures which generate poor places. In light of this temptation, a governmental analysis appears to offer a logical account of this rather partial approach to the vexatious 'urban question' (Lawless et al. 2009) that has troubled governments down the years as highlighted in Chapter 1.

The normative aspect of NDC has been reiterated throughout the book and it is clear that New Labour did not hesitate in asserting its vision of how 'communities' should look and behave. One explanation for implementing NDC in 'appropriate' areas therefore could be rooted in an aspiration to 'recreate community engagement' and 'foster moral dialogue' (Rose 2000: 1404) within excluded spaces. 'Community' then becomes a 'means' of government – unable in advanced liberal societies to overtly regulate its citizens – to instil social order and recast the terms of citizenship. As we have seen this can entail residents being co-opted into strategies of management and surveillance of their community and of each other (Flint 2003). If this analysis is accurate, then NDC was not about authentic 'empowerment' of residents, it was actually a mechanism for inscribing – to reiterate Rose – 'the norms of self control more deeply into the soul of each citizen' (2000: 1409). In addition, the models of NDC were not about recognising and responding to diversity and difference in neighbourhoods because:

> This version of the politics of community seeks to foreclose the problems of diversity by propagating a moral code justified by reference to values that purport to be timeless, natural, obvious, and incontestable. In operating at this moral pole ... the Third Way sets itself in opposition to the very autonomy it purports to respect' (Rose 2000: 1409).

Therefore, if we accept this argument, NDC functioned as a regulatory mechanism with prescriptions to construct the future trajectory for excluded areas and those who inhabit them in such a way that they generate sites of discipline and surveillance. Moreover, it identifies certain spaces as being more receptive to such strategies than others. The suggestion of this argument is that the state is, in effect, delegating control to non-state actors and entities, such as communities in the belief that order and individual conduct can be better maintained through the activation of citizens, than through its own activities, which are increasingly viewed as overbearing or inefficient. Therefore, concepts such as 'empowerment' in a regeneration context are inherently regulatory, evinced by the fact that they are heavily circumscribed by government-defined expectations about how agents should behave and should provide support for a model of governance conceived by government, but without participating in the conception process.

The governmentality perspective clearly originates from a different epistemological tradition than the 'sticking plaster' argument, but the conclusion is the same: citizens are being encouraged or constituted as local actors within 'geographies of responsibility' (Massey 2004) in which the identities of 'active' citizens – particularly for those residents in poor neighbourhoods – are increasingly configured as place bound. Therefore, ensuring that NDC spaces were coterminous with the needs and emotions of local residents was irrelevant as the regeneration process was about locating agents within responsible, self-governing territories that functioned in ways defined by central government. Indeed, clearly an effect of NDC was to lock residents into these socio-political formations, but governmentality only provides us with the analytical tools to identify this impulse, not the critical basis on which to understand or explain the tensions and disconnections highlighted here. This encapsulates the key problematic of this discussion: how to explain the ensnaring of citizens in restrictive formations, without recourse to theories of management or intended regulation.

In trying to think more broadly and navigate our way through this complicated terrain, we need to consider the arguments of the critical governance literature which suggests that processes of 'localisation' are occurring alongside a deepening of the control of the central state (Davies 2005). In particular, there are those who point to the emergence of 'meta-governance' (Jessop 2003) through which hierarchical power relations are maintained, structuring both the development and circumscribing of localised political projects (Whitehead 2003). This throws into question the authenticity of new governance spaces as sites of expanded citizen autonomy and raises the possibility of state control being augmented rather than disaggregated. It appears that for many in Salford, the NDC experience was an ambiguous one. The partnership itself was clearly allowed a certain level of autonomy in terms of priority setting and resource allocation and avenues for involving local residents were a central feature. However, it was destabilised by an uncertain and shifting central government policy architecture (see Lawless et al. 2009) and was subject to what we might consider a 'new science of metrics and measures' (Amin 2005: 620) – used by central government to performance manage policy initiatives. Furthermore, it seems evident that in Salford, as in other NDC areas, broader local, regional and national policy goals undermined or constrained the 'localist' integrity of programmes, with the housing redevelopment framework being the most controversial example in Salford. As such, residents in Salford experienced a simultaneous opening up and closing down of new citizenship possibilities. They were invited to engage with and participate in self-governing projects (some of which were dubious in their effect of facilitating notions of a unitary community voice or set of values). However, they also had to contend with the circumscribing of their empowerment by the predominance of NDC market-driven regeneration logic and injurious cultural and political neglect.

This literature is useful in trying to provide an account of NDC. It reflects the ambiguous, shifting nature of new governance spaces, which position citizens in difficult policy terrain both enhancing and restricting self-realisation. However, it is here that this contribution runs out of steam. My concern here has been to explain the disconnection between NDC rationality and my theorising of community, agency and exclusion and it was necessary to touch upon some important if familiar perspectives to colour this discussion. I accept that the structures and hierarchies of governance are important in understanding why citizens feel frustrated by projects like NDC, but they do not explain the failure of New Labour governments to understand how communities operate, thereby restricting and frustrating the exercise of greater citizen freedom. In addressing this failure I have constructed a binary between freedom, autonomy and justice for local residents with the citizenships on offer through governmentality, hierarchical governance or the localisation of neo-liberalism. These are vital perspectives, but the final part of my discussion will return to the citizenships offered by New Labour in order to provide further explanation of the lack and impact of NDC generated selfhoods.

NDC Citizenship – Where Did It Go Wrong?

Throughout this book, I have emphasised the role played by the reinterpretation of welfare by New Labour politicians and policymakers in shaping how governments under their stewardship sought to reimagine social citizenship. In understanding why NDC embodied and implemented limited models of community, agency and exclusion I think this position needs to be reasserted. To reiterate some of the arguments of Chapter 2, New Labour placed great stock in its ability to offer an empathetic reading of the needs and values of the poor. New Labour thought it had a recipe for success in excluded areas that comprised a workable, sustainable and beneficial package. NDC contained a normative agenda of the type alluded to above insofar as New Labour believed that if the conditions were right, participation, ownership, order and so on would be the inevitable result of NDC's presence. That is, New Labour appeared to believe these aspects of community and agency were lying latent in certain spaces and with a little government assistance would spring into life. Selected areas were rewarded with NDC funding because they were thought to deserve that opportunity for renewal and ownership as this was where the assistance or treatment was thought would work best. In other words, I would argue that New Labour conceived of the regeneration process as liberating rather than regulatory. Liberating for the 'decent' citizens who just needed a chance to participate in the governance of their locale and even liberating for those deviants who were the internal targets of 'strong communities' as they would be bound to the collective and taught the merits of responsible citizenship. Consideration is due here to New Labour's very deliberate attempt to avoid areas of overt conflict and division and reward 'correct' expressions of community (areas with relative homogeneity and consensus). That is, the selection of those areas with the 'best' chance of success and a return on government investment betrays an attempt to try and 'get it right' and suggests that policymakers believed they had minimised if not jettisoned the possibility that NDC zones were *also* contested and divided spaces. I would tentatively suggest that New Labour did not consciously set out to ensnare or hem local residents in restrictive socio-political formations. This does not excuse all of NDC's explicit goals however. In Salford, injurious developments were facilitated and problematic social divisions exploited – all as deliberate policy objectives. Nonetheless, the substance of my objections relates not just to the consequence of deliberate goals, but to the unintended consequences – the hidden injuries of New Labour's assumptions about poverty and community. Whilst attempting to devise interventions in poor neighbourhoods that allied government objectives of strengthened communities with resident needs and values is laudable to some degree, the fact remains that the NDC programmes *in their effects* functioned to neglect and obscure many local needs. This occurred in two main ways.

In the first instance, one offshoot of its attempt to construct community was actually to unwittingly sanction its contestation. NDC and its efforts to instil a community consciousness actually invited competing claims over 'communal' spaces and facilities because it misunderstood the fractured nature of the area. By *naming* the community it immediately constituted it as a site of struggle and negotiation that went beyond the imposition of the behavioural norms of the majority – one conflict it was prepared for. This, I would suggest, can be traced back to its lack of awareness of the heterogeneity in excluded spaces and the existence of multiple identities, norms and experiences and has two main consequences.

Firstly, one could argue that although NDC was trying to construct and impose an orderly community on unruly excluded terrain, its presence inadvertently opened a Pandora's box of local conflict by supplying a narrative or consciousness that residents exploit in their negotiation of community. That is, NDC encouraged claims to be made on people, public space and on how the area is 'renewed' and in so doing, undermined its own argument that such spaces are consensual. In the act of consultation, for example, it invited a range of opinions and tapped into the diversity of values held by residents, some of which will be in conflict with others – two outcomes of the consultation that it appeared to underestimate. In addition, by making funding available for projects and groups, there was an implicit contest over the allocation of resources and which ideas are 'rewarded'. This was probably best illustrated by the example of youth shelters where older residents objected to the plans for a designated youth space. This led to local police trying to intervene and manage the conflict and 'sell' the plans to those raising objections. Another example was the redevelopment plans. NDC were forced to both 'work' with residents who perceived the plans to be trespassing on 'their' community and mediate between those residents and estates who accepted the plans and pockets of resistance.

This also hints at a failure to understand how communities are 'made' – informally and shaped by relations of power. We saw in the previous chapter how certain groups in the zone were considered 'outsiders', (a phenomenon that the resident PA team also identified) and we know from other research accounts that the creation of insider/outsider divisions can be intrinsic to 'making' community. As shown in the previous chapter, 'space invaders' such as asylum seekers, students and private housing tenants were all subject to varying degrees of social closure in the NDC zone, at times manifesting in overt violence, but always reinforcing their status as 'outsiders'. Again, the arrival of NDC and its *naming* of community could be seen to have reinforced the creation of that divide by giving established or well-connected residents a resource with which to define the terms of community membership and construct a barrier between them and those they did not consider legitimate residents. As a result, it could have exacerbated social divisions within the space rather than building community and indirectly legitimise the exclusion of those groups and individuals from networks of affinity and support. Again, because of this disconnection between assumptions of unity and a divided reality, pressure was placed on local NDC partnerships to circumvent local divisions and to reach out to 'outsider' groups to try to ensure they are included in both the NDC process and integrated into the community.

This was the second consequence of 'naming' the community. NDC immediately defined tensions and conflict within the space as 'problems' *of* the community that required management strategies. In practice, this meant that NDC had to try to reach out to 'outsider' groups and try to resolve these various tensions, usually through liaising with advocacy and support groups. It also exposed the disconnection between hazy Government ideas about constructing 'community' and the reality facing those agencies on the ground that have to manage conflict between competing groups and the strategies adopted by individuals from those groups to safely negotiate their neighbourhood.

Another effect was to constitute excluded spaces as ones of conflict. In line with New Labour's models of community and agency, this meant encouraging residents to make claims on each other's behaviour in an ongoing dialogue with NDC, whether through meetings with workers and NDC police officers, or larger scale surveys and consultations. For example, I witnessed one residents meeting during which the local 'nuisance link' police officer addressed the audience and informed them of the availability of freepost 'antisocial behaviour forms' and urged residents to report such behaviour anonymously if necessary. The forms were also advertised in monthly NDC newsletters and shop windows. This type of policing of fellow residents' behaviour was constitutive of David Blunkett's 'Together Campaign' designed to 'provide local people with all they need to launch their own campaigns to galvanise their communities into action.' (Home Office 2004) Underwriting this vision of 'active' claim-making citizens, as we saw Chapter 2, is an analysis of community spaces (reflecting an analysis of society as a whole) as containing a behavioural fault line between the 'good', responsible majority and the deviant minority. Deriving from this analysis is a normative judgement that those 'good' community members should seek to moralise and reconstruct the deviant few, thereby enforcing the key reciprocal obligation of community membership – desistance from misbehaviour. This manifested in an assertion of 'decent', commonsense values and an upholding of social order by informing local police of 'bad' behaviour. This model of community enforcement also crept into reforms of local governance and implicated a range of service providers in the management of citizen behaviour. For example, in its White Paper *Building Communities, Beating Crime*, New Labour stated its intention to make public agencies more accountable to the public by giving,

> Local communities a formal way to request and ensure that action is taken by the
> police, local authorities and others in response to persistent anti-social behaviour
> or community safety problems. Or if that action is not taken – they will know
> why not publicly (Respect Task Force 2006: 28).

There were clear Foucauldian fingerprints on the implicating of public service staff to identify bad behaviour in this manner that Squires has described as a 'blurring of civil and criminal jurisdictions' (2006: 160). David Garland describes this panoptical dispersal of disciplinary possibilities as a 'responsibilisation strategy' which redistributes the 'task of crime control, rendering others responsible, multiplying the number of effective authorities, forming alliances ... The criminal justice state is, in this area at least, shedding its 'sovereign' style of governing by top-down command ...' (2001: 125). This approach is consistent with a shift identified by Fitzpatrick (2005b) from a top-down penal welfare state to governance 'at a distance.' That is, in order to manage risks and preserve the security of communities, residents are expected to 'become their own police force' (2005b: 169) and participate in the maintenance of social order. To some extent, this is intended to free up police time, but ultimately is about obviating the need for a police presence in the first place by instilling order. However, this trend must be contrasted with apparently increasing public calls for a 'visible police presence' on the streets (echoed by residents in the NDC zone). There is an apparent tension between public and bureaucratic understandings of effective policing.

To return to New Labour's analysis of a community fault line, it would seem that, predicated on this topography of social relations and behavioural codes, they believed NDC could confidently enter a community, provide the means of highlighting misbehaviour, and empower the 'good' residents (and local welfare agencies) who would then impose their moral authority on the rest. In fact, in the view of New Labour, there was little or no tension between facilitating contestation of this kind and building community; they were two sides of the same coin. However, this ideal moral community was undermined in Salford by the relational realities of living in such an area where a pervasive 'no grass' culture exists or is enforced. For example: 'Now as far those people are concerned it is crime and serious crime because they feel seriously intimidated and they are intimidated and you get the word 'grass' painted all over the place' ('Bill', resident and community representative, 21–60). Similarly:

> People won't come forward with evidence if they've seen somebody do something, erm, they wont give evidence and they won't give a statement ... There is a massive, erm, I've worked in quite a few places and I've never come across it like I have in Salford, there is a massive 'no grass' culture here ... You just don't say anything to anyone and that's sort of inbred and it's really difficult to overcome ... (NDC police sergeant).

Moreover, a consequence of New Labour's eagerness for facilitating claims on behaviour and encouraging the imposition of one set of norms over the other was that there appeared to be one group in the community who consistently suffered. Young people, as we have seen, relied on public space more than any other group and are subjected to more scrutiny than any other. New Labour took this up as one of its core themes in government, reiterating the need to tackle 'yob' behaviour.

According to one youth worker, as a consequence of this, New Labour successfully 'lowered tolerance levels' and 'widened the parameters of bad behaviour' with young people suffering as a result. For example: 'Kids have hung around street corners shops since Adam was a lad, but now that is called antisocial behaviour' ('Paul', youth worker). He told me of boys playing football in a local pub car park who were moved because patrons defined it as 'antisocial behaviour' and called the police. It was against this political and rhetorical backdrop that young people were problematised by older residents and had their claims on NDC arbitrated by other members of the 'community'. (Exemplified by the blocking of youth shelters in which adults mobilised a narrative of 'bad' behaviour to justify their obstinacy.) 'Paul' suggests that: 'A lot of people seem to forget that young people are part of the community, or don't want them part of the community. New Deal views young people as a threat rather than an asset' ('Paul', youth worker). Indeed, the first consultation of residents by the PA team contained 'youth' as a subcategory of 'community' issues to be addressed alongside transport, housing, environment and so on, immediately constructing this group as a concern for the community to consider.

This seems to be an example of where the disconnection has real implications for one section of the community. The reality of inviting claims on behaviour is that social divisions such as age will inform definitions of behaviour and morality and therefore the nature and extent of claims made. In addition, the process of 'making' community and deciding who is an 'insider' and 'outsider' may play its part in shaping definitions of 'good' behaviour and the problematising of certain groups. That is, making claims on young people may be less to do with conduct and more to do with social difference, underpinned by divisions of age, and which groups of residents want to be in the community under continual (re)creation.

Nevertheless, New Labour presumed an agreed behavioural code based on 'commonsense' and 'decency' – decoupled from any sense of social context or subjectivity. By contrast, I would suggest that there are in fact competing definitions of good conduct shaped by a range of social divisions including class, gender, ethnicity and age.[2] Moreover, New Labour's feverish commitment to making claims on bad behaviour was subjective and, as Squires has noted, 'the reaction and perception ... of third parties are central to its definition' (2006: 159). Clearly, this raises concerns about who is able to make 'stick' particular definitions of behaving antisocially. Introducing a racial dimension to the debate, Squires argues: '... the definitional ambiguities about what, exactly, constitutes ASB (antisocial behaviour) may reinforce racist and discriminatory interpretations of youthful behaviour' (2006: 161). The upshot of all this is that young people, less influential and less vocal in staking their claim for 'good' behaviour become the targets of the definitions of some adult residents who consider consumption of public space, usually in groups,

---

2   Indeed, one could argue that youth behaviour is often intended to subvert adult 'norms' creating a dichotomy that is irreconcilable with the notion of 'shared' norms and values and ensuring their exclusion from such a framework of social order.

dressing in casual wear and boisterousness as 'bad' behaviour. Young people who indulge in this sort of behaviour are then excluded from the making of community in a positive sense and become subject to further scrutiny and possibly measures of control. That is, there is a danger that certain brands of 'youth' are not considered a 'legitimate identity' (Furbey 1999: 438) when it comes to regeneration and participation. If young people are to be considered part of a community (which they should) this dynamic calls into question New Labour's assumption that contestations of behaviour are key to building community. In this case, facilitating such contestations, without considering the social differences that inform behaviour and morality and how different groups antagonise each other in their negotiated relationship (and in the 'making' of 'community') can lead to one group being consistently labelled as problematic. Practical exclusion is reinforced by a rhetorical exclusion from reciprocal citizenship in which politicians have made it plain that incivility entails a breaking of the contract between individuals and their community. Increasingly citizens owe duties to others in a contingent relationship, rather than to the state per se. If we consider Stuart White's position on 'fair reciprocity' (2003: 17), this provides a further tool for analysing this agenda. Leaving aside perpetrators of serious criminality (who we can assume have transgressed a line of generally acceptable conduct), if we accept that the enforcement of individual obligations and/ or punishment for non-contribution to the community (a non-contribution meaning, in this case, the failure to uphold social order by behaving in an antisocial manner) can only be justified if there is sufficient distributive justice and a fair allocation of opportunities, then perhaps we must accept Rob White's argument of the need for greater 'restorative social justice' (2003: 253). In trying to build behaviourist communities through naming and shaming strategies and operationalising some nebulous boundary to acceptable behaviour, it is arguable that it is less likely that conflict and contestation between groups can be resolved and understanding negotiated as it becomes too easy to define who is not making a contribution or who is not taking responsibility. This generates a rather positivist politics of behaviour wherein there is no account given of how behaviour is shaped through labelling processes or forms of policing or how behavioural norms may vary between groups or be contested. New Labour's community is then revealed as a rather limited framework through which to govern behaviour failing as it does to recognise the existence of processes of social division, defended space and marginalisation, and de-politicising as it does concepts of 'appropriate' conduct and performance. This is a framework in which the socioeconomic status or political resources of your neighbour are rendered irrelevant – what matters is they are not a 'nuisance' or a 'nightmare' as you define it.

Of course, government may defend this process by arguing that young people (indeed everyone) should be subject to scrutiny and stress the importance of protecting the security of well-behaved residents and this is fine to a point. There is no merit in defending criminal or genuinely threatening behaviour, particularly when certain areas experience the accumulation of such behaviours over time, but the point is the tendency to problematise youth per se with little or no recognition that definitions of 'good' conduct and 'respectability' are not fixed but fluid and socially shaped. Furthermore, there is a hollowness to the concept of 'antisocial' behaviour that reflects a 'victory of behaviourism over social positivism' (Squires 2006: 157). In other words, behaviour is stripped of context to become about 'motivation and intentions' (2006: 157) rather than possible causes that require support rather than punishment.

As a result, it has to be said that New Labour's belief that the construction of community includes encouraging residents to make claims on each other risks neglecting existing relations of power and influence and legitimising the policing of certain groups whose behaviour is perceived (in the eyes of the dominant (adult) beholders) to be deviant. The attempt to create community through behavioural and moral unity fails to recognise the complexity of social groupings and the intersection of power and social division that produce a hierarchy of definitions of 'good conduct' therein. Finally, it risks appearing like a cynical attempt to appease the supposed 'respectable' members of that grouping by 'empowering' them to effect social closure (and possibly exclusion) on others.

Conclusion

The purpose of this chapter has been to explore different perspectives on the disconnection identified between NDC rationality for poor spaces and my accounts of community, agency and exclusion. This has led us to examine some important critical analyses of state-directed regeneration projects. However, whilst each of these has some bearing on how we can understand the NDC, I suggested a somewhat more prosaic explanation. Whilst I think we can identify aspects of NDC which were designed to re-orientate poor spaces towards being consensual, socio-political products, a significant component of this derived from an attempt to provide citizens with a model of community relations and inclusionary experience that they were assumed to covet. Some might consider this a disingenuous project of manufactured consent for poverty management, but having unpacked the New Labour approach to the social and welfare governance, I maintain that NDC was an attempt to deliver renewal and responsibility in ways that 'respectable' citizens wanted and deserved. However, my argument is that New Labour thought they could somehow skirt round material inequality by sublimating it to questions of the social, community and their associated cohesion and regeneration. However, as I have shown, communities are products framed by materiality and vulnerable to state-sponsored attempts at 'empowerment'. NDC citizens were often ensnared in damaging regenerative projects made worse by the discursive constraints provided by New Labour's therapeutic modality of government that attempted to empathize, understand and 'unleash' local 'potential' but which often compounded and layered the exclusion of the NDC urban poor. At root, I would suppose that this failure reflected New Labour's broader tendency towards rather anaemic, de-politicised accounts of social change, fearful as it was of the conflict or jeopardy generated by holistic accounts of and challenges to social division. This manifested in the offer of consensual selfhoods for those most aware of the vagaries and ruptures that poverty can engender. The danger was always that where these were challenged, some citizens would find themselves excluded from regenerative discourses, constructed as 'undeserving' of New Labour's largesse. Once again, those with most to overcome were too often left to negotiate and surmount challenges not of their own making.

Chapter 8
Concluding Thoughts

Introduction

There are two key arguments around which this discussion has been based. Firstly, that to some degree NDC was shaped by a set of concepts derived from the New Labour political project and consequent reformulations of the welfare state. I asserted that the rationality that underpinned NDC can be traced back to three key principles underpinning the wider 'project' – community, opportunity and responsibility. These governing precepts seeped into the regeneration policy arena as New Labour sought to refurbish some of the poorest, excluded extremities of the social body through a combination of reconstructing individual behaviour and the delivery of extra and better resources. I argued that this chimed with a policy dynamic occurring within and beyond New Labour's time in office that saw local territories become increasingly drawn into public policy arenas as partners and co-producers of welfare. These two forces combined to produce NDC spaces that were intriguing experiments in which new citizenships were constituted. As local residents were drawn in as participants in localised governance, they were also forced to negotiate a set of assumptions about their identity, values, needs and voices bound up with the logic and direction of NDC programmes designed to regenerate the physical and cultural scaffolding of their neighbourhoods.

Secondly, it was argued that NDCs framework or rationality for refurbishment could be problematised on the basis of a lack of awareness or sensitivity to the complexities of the terrain that it sought to engage. Consequently, it was suggested that this lack of awareness/sensitivity, in addition to some very deliberate governing techniques, created potential or real tensions in the refurbishment project envisaged by New Labour. Ultimately, I argue that local citizens have not been enabled to embark on satisfactory 'journeys of empowerment' (Warren-Adamson, cited in Dinham 2005: 303), or select and pursue what Brenner and Theodore call 'developmental pathways' (2002: 342) at the local level. I suggested that this was not so much because NDC was a strategy for managing the poor by shoe-horning them into specified socio-political configurations, or offering limited opportunities for empowerment. My argument rested on the belief that NDC restricted and frustrated its resident citizens because it functioned in such a way that many residents could not or did not want to participate in the regeneration process. Whether that process was authentic, meaningful or genuine is difficult to discern and was not the main preoccupation of this discussion. To some degree, I utilise NDC as something of a heuristic or framework by which I explore the rhythms and complexities of that most maligned of sociological concepts: community. My analysis of NDC is one that draws on a 'search' for community (Brent 2009) and touches upon questions of epistemology, ontology and methodology in the course of that search. I politicise community in such a manner to try and understand its ruptures and tensions and NDC plays a vital role in that process. Of course, this opens me up to criticism of how I handle NDC and whether it can bear the weight of critique that I place upon it. To some degree it probably cannot and having wrestled with this point for some time, I have concluded that this is a valid, though tangential perspective since NDC is constructed here as a rationality – an embodiment of ideas, assumptions, imaginaries and prescriptions that New Labour sought to deploy in poor neighbourhoods. NDC as practice is less important than NDC as site, space, modality or discourse in this discussion and it is in the interstices that these generated and the new citizenships that emerged that I have sought to situate and expand my critical take on New Labour.

How the Book Unfolded

Whilst Chapter 1 located NDC within a lineage of poverty programmes driven by a policy discourse preoccupied with poor spaces, Chapter 2 attempted to trace its origins to the wider New Labour welfare reform project. It was my argument that NDC reflected both a construction of poor areas as a policy 'problem' and the *prescription* applied in the course of addressing this 'problem.' The objective of Chapter 2 was to explore the genesis of this prescription and theorise its relationship with broader New Labour concepts and analyses. It was asserted that a substantial part of New Labour's governing project was about reforming welfare systems and reframing the relationship between citizen and state.

Whilst it was noted that Giddens' 'post-traditional' society analysis was key to understanding New Labour's reform of the welfare state, the core principles woven throughout much of the reform agenda were identified as: community, opportunity and responsibility. New Labour's social vision was underpinned by these three concepts that acted as both policy objectives and organising precepts. It was argued that New Labour sought to both provide opportunities and expand the attendant responsibilities of citizens on the basis of 'community' membership. Not only were we expected to participate in economic and political life, but we also had a crucial role to play in maintaining the moral fabric of the community – so must participate in the public negotiation of behavioural standards, what Flint and Nixon have described as a call for 'positive action' focused on 'the governance of others' rather than simply a personal, passive 'desistance from incivility' (2006: 952). A responsible citizen should do more than look at their own behaviour and should try to shape the character of others.

This process is also partly constitutive of what became known as 'active' citizenship – participation in the civic life of the community where members are involved in constructing the public realm through volunteering, involvement in local politics and social entrepreneurialism amongst other things. It also underpinned New Labour's conception of the community as one that contains a crucial dividing line between the decent majority and the antisocial or deviant minority. To overcome this division 'decent' members need to take responsibility for policing the behaviour of the deviants in their midst. The identification of this welfare reform agenda is crucial for understanding NDC. I have argued that the prescription for poor areas devised by New Labour can be traced back to these broader political and philosophical positions.

Community in the context of NDC was identified as the guiding principle for the refurbishment process in the sense that NDC represented an attempt to mould a community out of malleable socially excluded terrain entailing the allocation of responsibilities for residents and the construction of an identity for chosen spaces. Community underpinned the future trajectory of NDC areas – how New Labour wanted the areas to emerge post-NDC 'treatment'.

Clearly, part of the community vision was a model of individual agency propounded by NDC. This model related to the wider importance attached by New Labour to responsibility and manifested at the local level via NDC as a range of duties expected of residents in the course of building the community. Specific forms of participation were expected in the course of 'animating' the community to be active, responsible local citizens. Again, New Labour's model of agency presumed that there to be a majority of residents ready and willing to participate in local decision-making and service delivery. NDC's role was to provide the opportunities and avenues for this activity to flourish, including the spread of 'respect' and decent values. The final ingredient inherent in NDC related to exclusion and was linked with the wider concern for providing opportunities for citizens. Whereas the models of agency and community shared some degree of concern about changing behaviour and cultures of poor areas, the model of exclusion represented the need to refurbish the physical and political context of these areas.

Having theorised the conceptual framework of NDC and established how each model manifests as a set of aspirations for residents and their community, Chapters 3 to 5 shifted the focus of the discussion onto the discordant literature so central to the research supporting my arguments. After exploring some of the critical assessments of New Labour and its rhetoric and welfare reforms, these chapters proceeded to focus on the three models of agency, community and exclusion. With reference to a range of literature and data from the field, I attempted to problematise the analyses and objectives inherent in each model and develop research questions on which to base my enquiry. To begin, it was re-iterated that local interest in NDC was rather limited and that involvement in the 'community' per se was mixed, with some respondents mentioning the importance of their immediate street or block, but declaring little contact or affinity with the 'community' defined by NDC. Attendance at residents and tenants meetings was found to be relatively high, but distinctly gendered. Moreover, territorial division was found to influence the priorities of associations and provide a division that cut across the NDC zone as a whole. In terms of community and the extent of contestation, it was argued that social divisions undermined the pockets of community engagement that do exist. Data was described that illustrated conflicts between residents needs and values relating to local policing strategies and redevelopment plans. There was also evidence to suggest that the presence of 'outsider' groups (what I termed 'space invaders' – students, asylum seekers and transient private housing tenants) was the cause of contestations of space and identity. Finally, evidence was described that illustrated how some residents have clashed over the use of physical space within the community, generally manifesting in a conflict between young people who consider themselves reliant on public space, and older people who define such occupation as a nuisance to be controlled. It was my contention that the combination of data around contestations and divisions produced a substantial case for questioning New Labour's model of community as either being in existence, or the possibility of it being created. The final body of data to be discussed was that relating to exclusion and how residents experience it. In response, it was suggested that three distinct processes were in operation that shaped experiences of exclusion in differing ways. Firstly, evidence was offered to suggest that needs were shaped by the interaction of poor local services with social location or division. Secondly, it was argued that within a defined space such as this, that there were simply a range of needs exhibited by different individuals and groups to conduct their everyday lives. Finally, a relational dimension to the configuration of needs was explored. This entailed recounting evidence that showed how social relations could shape or reinforce experiences of exclusion through the existence of territorialism and the maintenance of insider/outsider boundaries.

The combination of data explored in these chapters was not suggested to be an all-encompassing account of community experiences and dynamics, but nonetheless to offer evidence of contested and heterogeneous terrain that raised concerns about NDC's awareness and sensitivity to the community it sought to regenerate. It appeared to underwrite a disconnection between how New Labour conceived of excluded spaces and the realities of socially excluded communities. This disconnection was discussed in Chapter 7 and distilled into several key themes by which to reflect upon NDC. Firstly, it was asserted that given the contested nature of the community under study, it was necessary to question why it was selected as being 'suitable' for NDC funding.

Secondly, the disconnection between NDC rationality and reality was discussed in detail in Chapter 7 with reference to the implications of two key components of New Labour's NDC project. Firstly, it was argued that the belief that it is the duty of government to facilitate the assertion of 'decent' values and the policing of deviancy within 'communities' actually has a disproportionate effect on young people who are most likely to be constructed as deviant or antisocial. The second implication identified was in New Labour's apparent belief in the benign presence of NDC partnerships. It was suggested here that NDC's presence actually functioned to inadvertently create conflict as soon as it 'names' the space as a community. Consequently, claims are invited on territory that can manifest in social closure and on NDC resources that can result in in-fighting as has been reportedly the case in a number of NDC areas (See for example, Weaver 2002; Power and Wilmott 2005).

Chapter 7 also included a discussion of how best to understand NDC and the intentionality behind its application: was NDC about managing or regulating excluded communities? If so, empowerment rhetoric was indeed disingenuous because NDC was predominantly about maintaining the status quo and creating communities that were sites of discipline and surveillance. However, whilst I recognised that NDC did contain elements of a normative vision, I argued that rather than being a sinister attempt to regulate poor people and spaces, New Labour conceived of NDC as liberating and as a reward for 'deserving' citizens. The problem was that when its prescriptions – its liberating project – are exposed as flawed, NDC begins to look like a crude attempt to impose its own vision and control excluded spaces.

Conclusion

These examples of disconnection between the reality of living in excluded areas with an NDC presence, and the imagined prescriptions found within the NDC rationale revealed some very important flaws in the NDC project for refurbishing poor neighbourhoods. Whilst much further research needs to be conducted to better understand some key dynamics and effects of NDC policies, I would argue that the problems outlined here represent a case against NDC that must be balanced against the positive practical developments it has helped initiate in many areas, including Salford. It seems clear that in some key respects, NDC was not an appropriate basis on which to address and manage neighbourhood exclusion. In fact, for some residents, NDC functioned to reinforce or neglect their exclusion. Clearly, we need to be careful not to unify or to collectivise NDC's failures; there is an equal and opposite danger of assuming we can generalise from the experiences of some residents to an encompassing assessment of NDC's impact. If this book has achieved anything, I hope it has been to trouble assumptions of unified social experience and it should be asserted at this point that NDC was a positive experience for some residents who did indeed feel that New Labour was responding to their desire to participate more effectively in their locality. As ever, NDC was a complex, inconsistent intervention in people's lives and reactions and experiences will always be frustratingly difficult to neatly define or map. Perhaps there is a need, following Jessop, to accept that all modes of governance have a tendency to fail and that NDC partnerships should be have been encouraged to 'develop self-reflexive means of coping with the failures, contradictions, dilemmas and paradoxes' (2003: 10).

Nevertheless, there is a need to work through the difficulties of 'new localism' (Ellison and Ellison 2006) and unpack discourses of freedom and empowerment which look set to continue to 'people' new governance practices. From a policy perspective, it appears that until such time as genuine and more realistic commitments to the local level can be formulated, policy interventions in excluded spaces will continue to look towards 'community' as a policy solution, but without supplying the requisite means or capacity for addressing its problems and limitations. This may mean an exacerbation of local conflicts in the absence of any genuine local power or control to shape agenda and open up opportunities for local development projects to mediate and resolve contestations. It may also mean that people who inhabit the spaces identified by the regeneration policy radar continue to be subjects of policy who must respond to government imaginations of community, rather than developing future plans of their own. That is to say that whilst the discussion here has been focussed on disrupting unified notions of the local, this is not to deny the possibility of empowering organic movements for change. It should be clear that the preoccupation here has been to explore how resident citizens navigate socio-political formations that they do not recognise, trust or respect, not to dismiss the potential for transformative projects that may well mobilise understandings of community to invest their efforts with meaning and form. If politicians want to continue to try and generate community, perhaps they will need to explore an 'agonistic' politics (Amin 2005) that relies on recognising that difference is the fulcrum of community, not its downfall. Just as top-down policies can be disempowering for local citizens, bottom-up approaches are not without their problems if they accompany simplistic assumptions of homogeneity and cohesion (Craig 2007: 340). These problems are intensified if there is a failure to adequately theorise how local spaces function as constellations of needs, identities and forms of agency.

There are two key points to this final critique therefore. Firstly, despite its attempts to avoid division and disorder by applying NDC to specified areas disaggregated to a level of 4,000 or so households, it still appears that New Labour neglected the temporal and relational dynamics that (re)create local community space. Secondly, this lack of understanding of residents' lives means New Labour can be accused of undermining the potential of citizens to determine their own lives whilst expecting that they will participate in specified ways in their communities and legitimise the government's regeneration programme. In light of this, it is perhaps unsurprising that several NDCs were characterised by resistance and tensions (Weaver 2002) as residents responded to what is a frustratingly contradictory approach to regenerating people and spaces. Ultimately, it demonstrated a lack of regard for human agency by pulling residents in two directions at once – placing new demands, whilst failing to supply good enough opportunities. Not just opportunities through improved schooling, employment options or welfare support, but an understanding of citizens' wellbeing that takes proper account of their need for autonomy and self-realisation. This 'deal', it may be recalled, was New Labour's article of faith, but in the context of NDC, it was one that was too often skewed away from citizens' best interests. Whilst, it would be unfair to suggest that New Labour's attempts to remake community were inherently disciplinary, regulatory projects, the failures outlined here meant that all too often the poor continued to be ensnared in models of social being and change redolent of the more pernicious examples of regulatory public welfare down the years. This, I have argued, derived from an inability or unwillingness to conceive of fractured welfare subjects or spaces and injurious legacies of political neglect and social harm. New Labour had something of a consistent and genuine vision of welfare citizenship, but it was one that relied upon half-formed accounts of the social and an elision of difference and difficulty, ultimately generating ever-decreasing complexes of citizen freedom.

Bibliography

Alcock, P. 2004. Participation or pathology: contradictory tensions in area-based policy. *Social Policy and Society*, 3(2), 87–96.

Amin, A. 2002. Ethnicity and the multicultural city: living with diversity. *Environment and Planning*, 34(6), 959–80.

Amin, A. 2005. Local community on trial. *Economy and Society* 34(4), 612–33.

Atkinson, R. 2003. Addressing social exclusion through community involvement in community regeneration, in *Urban Renaissance? New Labour, Community and Urban Policy*, edited by R. Imrie and M. Raco. Bristol: Policy Press, 101–20.

Atkinson, P. and Kintrea, K. 2001. Disentangling area effects: evidence from deprived and non-deprived neighbourhoods. *Urban Studies*, 38(12), 2277–98.

Barnes. M., Newman, J., Knops, A. and Sullivan, H. 2003. Constituting 'the public' in public participation. *Public Administration*, 81(2), 379–99.

Bauman, Z. 1993. *Postmodern Ethics*. Oxford: Blackwell.

Bauman, Z. 2000. Social issues of law and order. *British Journal of Criminology*, 40, 205–21.

Bauman, Z. 2001. *Community: Seeking Safety in an Insecure World*. Oxford: Blackwell.

BBC Newsnight. 2003. *Report on NDC*, 7 August.

Beck, U. 1992. *Risk Society*. London: Sage.

Bell, D. 1998. Residential Community Associations: Community or Disunity? in *The Essential Communitarian Reader*, edited by A. Etzioni. Oxford: Rowman and Littlefield, 167–76.

Bell, C. and Newby, H. 1971. *Community Studies*. London: Allen and Unwin.

Benn, M. 2000. New Labour and social exclusion, *Political Quarterly*, 71(3), 309–18.

Bennington, J. and Donnison, D. 1999. New Labour and social exclusion: the search for a third way – or just 'gliding the ghetto' again? in *Social Policy Review 11*, edited by H. Dean and R. Woods. Luton: Social Policy Association.

Beresford, P. 2001. Service users, social policy and the future of welfare. *Critical Social Policy*, 21(4), 494–512.

Bergman, J. 1995. Social exclusion in Europe: policy context and analytical framework, in *Beyond the Threshold: The Measurement and Analysis of Social Exclusion*, edited by G. Room. Bristol: Policy Press, 10–28.

Blair, T. 1996. *New Britain: My Vision of a Young Country*. London: Fourth Estate.

Blair, T. 1998. *The Third Way: New Politics for the New Century*. London: Fabian Society.

Blair, T. 2001. Opportunity for all, responsibility from all: a new commitment to neighbourhood renewal. Speech at the launch of the National Strategy for Neighbourhood Renewal, 15 January.

Blair, T. 2002. *BBC Newsnight interview.* 16 May.

Blair, T. 2003. The saving grace of the baby bond. *The Guardian,* 10 April. Available at: http://www.guardian.co.uk/politics/2003/apr/10/budget2003. policy [Accessed 1 September 2009].

Blair, T. 2004. A new consensus on law and order. Speech at the launch of the Home Office and Criminal Justice System strategic plans, 19 July.

Blears, H. 2003. *Communities in Control: Public Services and Local Socialism.* London: Fabian Society.

Blears, H. 2008. Introduction to *Communities in Control: Real People, Real Power.* London: The Stationery Office.

Blunkett, D. 2002. Speech to 'Parent and Child 2002' – International Conference on Adolescence, National Parenting and Family Institute. London, 18 April.

Boeck, T. and Fleming, J. 2005. Social policy – a help or hindrance to social capital? *Social Policy and Society,* 4(3), 259–70.

Bornat, J. 1997. Representations of Community, in *Community Care: A Reader 2nd Edition,* edited by J. Bornat et al. London: Macmillan.

Bourdieu, P. 1991. *Language and Symbolic Power.* Cambridge: Harvard University Press.

Braham, P. and Jones, L. (eds). 2002. *Social Differences and Divisions.* Oxford: Blackwell.

Brenner, N. and Theodore, N. 2002. Preface: From the 'New Localism' to the spaces of neoliberalism. *Antipode,* 34(3), 341–47.

Brent, J. 1997. Community without unity, in *Contested Communities,* edited by P. Hoggett. Bristol: Policy Press.

Brent, J. 2009. *In Search of Community.* Bristol: Policy Press.

Brickell, P. 2000. *People before Structures: Engaging in Communities in Regeneration.* Demos pamphlet.

Bridge, G. and Watson, S. 2002. Lest Power be Forgotten: networks, division and difference in the city. *The Sociological Review,* 50(4), 505–22.

Brock, K. and McGee, R. (eds). 2002. *Knowing Poverty: Critical Reflections on Participatory Research and Policy.* London: Earthscan.

Brown, G. 1999. Speech at Sure Start conference, 7 July. Available at: http://archive.treasury.gov.uk/speech/cx70799.html [Accessed 16 April 2008].

Brown, G. 2000a. Speech to the Children and Young Person's Unit conference, 15 November. Available at: http://www.hm-treasury.gov.uk/press_129_00.htm [Accessed 16 April 2008].

Brown, G. 2000b. Speech to the Child Poverty Action Group's poverty conference, 15 May. Available at: http://webarchive.nationalarchives.gov.uk/+/http://www.hm-treasury.gov.uk/newsroom_and_speeches/press/2000/press_62_00.cfm [Accessed 1 February 2010].

Brown, G. 2002. Speech to the Urban Summit in Birmingham, 1 November Available at: http://www.hm-treasury.gov.uk/press_113_02.htm [Accessed 14 October 2009].

Burden, T., Cooper, C. and Petrie, S. 2000. *'Modernising' Social Policy: Unravelling New Labour's Welfare Reforms*. Aldershot: Ashgate.

Burney, E. 2005. *Making People Behave*. Cullompton: Willan Publishing.

Cameron, D. 2009. The Big Society, Hugo Young Lecture, 10 September. Available at: http://www.conservatives.com/News/Speeches/2009/11/David_Cameron_ The_Big_Society.aspx [Accessed 11 November 2009].

Cammack, P. 2004. Gidden's way with words, in *The Third Way and Beyond: Criticisms, Futures and Alternatives*, edited by S. Hale, W. Leggett and L. Martell. Manchester: Manchester University Press, 151–66.

Campbell, B. 1993. *Goliath: Britain's Dangerous Places*. London: Methuen.

Carson, W.G. and Wiles, P. (eds). 1971. *Crime and Delinquency in Britain: Sociological Readings*. Glasgow: Martin Robertson and Co.

Centre for Social Justice. 2006. *Breakdown Britain*. London.

Charlestown and Lower Kersal NDC Partnership. 2001a. *Salford New Deal for Communities Delivery Plan 2001–2011*. Salford.

Charlestown and Lower Kersal NDC Partnership. 2001b. *NDC Interim Management Arrangements 2001–2002*. Salford.

Charlestown and Lower Kersal NDC Partnership. 2003a. *Managing for Results, a performance management report and improvement plan*. Salford.

Charlestown and Lower Kersal NDC Partnership. 2003b. *Salford New Deal for Communities Delivery Plan 2003–2004*. Salford.

Charlestown and Lower Kersal NDC Partnership. 2004. *Salford New Deal for Communities Delivery Plan 2004/05 – 2006/07*. Salford.

Charlestown and Lower Kersal NDC Partnership. 2005. Annual Report 2004/05. Salford.

Charlestown and Lower Kersal NDC Partnership. 2009. Programme Evaluation Report 2008/09. Salford.

Clarke, J., Lewis, G. and Gewirtz, S. (eds). 2000. *Rethinking Social Policy*. London: Sage.

Clarke, J. 2005. New Labour's citizens: activated, empowered, responsibilised, abandoned? *Critical Social Policy*, 25(4), 447–63.

Clegg, D. 2005. A rootless third way: a continental European perspective on New Labour's welfare state revisited, in *Social Policy Review 17*, edited by M. Powell, L. Bauld and K. Clarke. Bristol: Policy Press.

Cochrane, A. 2000. New Labour, new urban policy? in *Social Policy Review 12*, edited by H. Dean and R. Woods. Newcastle: Social Policy Association, 184– 202.

Cochrane, A. 2003. New Urban Policy? In *Urban Renaissance*, edited by R. Imrie and M. Raco. Bristol: Policy Press, 223–34.

Cohen, N. 2003. *Pretty Straight Guys*. London: Faber & Faber.

Community Development Project (CDP). 1977. *Gilding the Ghetto: The State and the Poverty Experiments.* London: CDP.

Corner, J. and Pels, D. (eds). 2003. *Media and the Restyling of Politics.* London: Sage.

Craig, G. and Mayo, M. 1995. Community participation and empowerment: the human face of structural adjustment or tools for democratic transformation, in *Community Empowerment: A Reader in Participation and Development,* edited by G. Craig and M. Mayo. London: Zed Books, 1–11.

Craig, G. 2007. Community capacity-building: something old, something new...? *Critical Social Policy,* 27(3), 335–59.

Centre for Regional Economic and Social Research (CRESR). 2003. *NDC National Evaluation: pen portraits of the 39 partnerships.* London: DCLG.

CRESR 2009a. *Four years of change: understanding the experiences 2002–2006 New Deal for Communities Panel main report.* London: DCLG.

CRESR 2009b. *Improving outcomes? Engaging local communities in the NDC programme.* London: DCLG.

CRESR 2009c. *The NDC programme. Outputs and expenditure over the period 1999–2007.* London: DCLG.

Crow, G. and Allan, G. 1994. *Community Life: An Introduction to Local Social Relations.* Hemel Hempstead: Harvester Wheatsheaf.

Crow, G. 2002 Community Studies: Fifty Years of Theorisation, *Sociological Research Online,* 7(3). Available at: http://www.socresonline.org.uk/7/3/crow.html [Accessed 2 March 2010].

Daly, M. 2003. Governance and Social Policy. *Journal of Social Policy,* 32(1), 113–28.

Davies, J. 2001. *Partnerships and Regimes: The Politics of Urban Regeneration in the UK.* Aldershot: Ashgate.

Davies, J. 2005. Local governance and the dialectics of hierarchy, market and network. *Policy Studies,* 26(3/4), 311–35.

Day, G. 1996. Community, locality and social identity, in *Developments in Sociology,* edited by M. Haralambos. Ormskirk: Causeway Press.

Day, G. 2006. *Community and Everyday Life.* Oxford: Routledge.

Day, G. and Murdoch, J. 1993. Locality and Community: coming to terms with place, *The Sociological Review,* 41(1), 82–111.

Department for Communities and Local Government (DCLG). 2008a. *The NDC national evaluation: the six case studies, an introduction,* London: TSO.

DCLG. 2008b. *Communities in control; real people, real power.* London: TSO

DCLG. 2010. *Smarter Government.* London: TSO.

Deacon, A. 1998. The Green Paper on Welfare Reform: a case for enlightened self-interest? *Political Quarterly,* 69(3), 306–11.

Deacon, A. 2000. Learning from the US? The influence of American ideas upon 'new Labour' thinking on welfare reform. *Policy and Politics,* 28(1), 5–18.

Deacon, A. 2002a. Echoes of Sir Keith? New Labour and the Cycle of Disadvantage. *Benefits,* 10(3), 179–84.

Deacon, A. 2002b. *Perspectives on Welfare*. Buckingham: Open University Press.

Deacon, A. 2003. Levelling the playing field, activating the players': New Labour and the 'cycle of disadvantage. *Policy and Politics*, 31(2), 123–27.

Deacon, A. 2004. Justifying conditionality: The case of anti-social tenants. *Housing Studies,* 19(6), 911–26.

Deacon, A. and Mann, K. 1997. Moralism and Modernity: The paradox of New Labour thinking on welfare. *Benefits*, 20, 2–6.

Deacon, A and Mann, K. 1999. Agency, Modernity and Social Policy. *Journal of Social Policy* 28(3), 413–35.

Dean, M. 1999. *Governmentality: Power and Rule in Modern Society*. London: Sage.

Dean, J. and Hastings, A. 2000. Challenging images: housing estates, stigma and regeneration. Available at: http://www.jrf.org.uk/sites/files/jrf/jr089-housing-estates-regeneration.pdf [Accessed 16 January 2010].

Dicks, B., Waddington, D. and Critcher, C. 1998. Redundant men and overburdened women, in *Men, Gender Divisions and Welfare*, edited by J. Popay, J. Hearn and J. Edwards. London: Routledge, 287–311.

Dinham, A. 2005. Empowered or over-powered? The real experiences of local participation in the UK's New Deal for Communities. *Community Development Journal*, 40(3), 301–12.

Dobbs, L. and Moore, C. 2002. Engaging Communities in Area-Based Regeneration: The Role of Participatory Evaluation. *Policy Studies*, 23(3/4), 157–71.

Docherty, I., Goodlad, R., and Paddison, R. 2001. Civic culture, community and citizen participation in contrasting neighbourhoods. *Urban Studies*, 38(12), 2225–50.

Driver, S. 2004. North Atlantic drift: welfare reform and 'Third Way' politics of New Labour and the New Democrats, in *The Third Way and Beyond: Criticisms, Futures and Alternatives*, edited by S. Hale, W. Leggett and L. Martell. Manchester: Manchester University Press, 31–47.

Driver, S. and Martell, L. 1998. *New Labour: Politics after Thatcherism*. Cambridge: Polity Press.

Driver, S. and Martell, L. 2000. Left, Right and the Third Way. *Policy and Politics* 28(2), 147–61.

Driver, S. and Martell, L. 2002. *Blair's Britain*. Cambridge: Polity Press.

Durose, C., Greasley, S. and Richardson, L. (eds). 2009. *Changing Local Governance, Changing Citizens*. Bristol: Policy Press.

Department of Work and Pensions (DWP). 2002. *Opportunity for All – Fourth Annual Report*. London: TSO.

Department for Social Security (DSS). 1998. *Green Paper on Welfare Reform*. London: DSS.

Dwyer, P. 1998. Conditional citizens? Welfare rights and responsibilities in the late 1990s. *Critical Social Policy*, 18(4), 493–514.

Dwyer, P. 2000. *Welfare Rights and Responsibilities: Contesting Social Citizenship.* Bristol: Policy Press.

Dwyer, P. and Brown, D. 2005. Meeting Basic Needs? Forced Migrants and Welfare. *Social Policy and Society,* 4(4), 369–80.

East, L. 2002. Regenerating health in communities: voices from the inner city. *Critical Social Policy,* 22(2), 147–73.

Edwards, J. 1997. Urban policy: the victory of form over substance. *Urban Studies,* 34(5–6), 825–43.

Edwards, J., Oakley, A. and Popay, J. 1999. Service Users' and Providers' Perspectives on Welfare Needs, in *Welfare Research: A Critical Review,* edited by F. Williams, J. Popay and A. Oakley. London: UCL Press.

Elias, N. and Scotson, J. 1994. *The Established and the Outsiders.* 2nd Edition. London: Sage.

Ellison, N. and Ellison, S. 2006. Creating Opportunity for All? New Labour, New Localism and the Opportunity Society. *Social Policy and Society,* 5(3), 337–48.

Elshtain, J. Bethke. 1998. Democracy and the Politics of Difference, in *The Essential Communitarian Reader,* edited by A. Etzioni. Oxford: Rowman and Littlefield, 259–68.

Engels, F. 1969. *The Condition of the Working Class in England.* London: Panther.

Etzioni, A. 1993. *The Spirit of Community.* London: Fontana Press.

Etzioni, A. 1997. *The New Golden Rule.* London: Profile.

Etzioni, A. 1998. The Responsive Communitarian Platform: Rights and Responsibilties, in *The Essential Communitarian Reader,* edited by A. Etzioni. Oxford: Rowman and Littlefield, 1–2.

Fairclough, N. 2000. *New Labour, New Language?* London: Routledge.

Ferguson, H. 2003. Welfare, Social Exclusion and Reflexivity: The case of child and woman protection. *Journal of Social Policy,* 32(2), 199–216.

Finlayson, A. 1999. Third Way Theory. *The Political Quarterly,* 70(3), 271–79.

Fitzpatrick, S. and Jones, A. 2005. Pursuing social justice or social cohesion? Coercion in Street Homelessness policies in England. *Journal of Social Policy,* 34(3), 389–406.

Fitzpatrick, T. 2005a. The fourth attempt to construct a politics of welfare obligations. *Policy and Politics,* 33(1), 15–32.

Fitzpatrick, T. 2005b. *New Theories of Welfare.* Basingstoke: Palgrave Macmillan.

Flint, J. 2003. Housing and Ethopolitics: constructing identities of active consumption and responsible community. *Economy and Society,* 32(3), 611–29.

Flint, J. and Nixon, J. 2006. Governing Neighbours: antisocial behaviour orders and new forms of regulation conduct in the UK. *Urban Studies,* 43(5/6), 939–55.

Foley, P. 1999. New Labour: New Deal for Communitites? *Public Money and Management*, 1, 7–8.

Foley, P. and Martin, S. 2000. A new deal for the community? Public participation in regeneration and local service delivery. *Policy and Politics*, 28(4), 479–91.

Forrest, R. and Kearns, A. 2001. Social cohesion, social capital and the neighbourhood. *Urban Studies*, 38(23), 2125–43.

Frankenberg, R. 1965. *Communities in Britain*. Middlesex: Penguin.

Fremeaux, I. 2005. New Labour's appropriation of the concept of community: a critique. *Community Development Journal*, 40(3), 265–74.

Frow, E. and Frow, R. 1984. *Radical Salford: Episodes in Labour History*. Salford: Working Class Movement Library.

Furbey, R. 1999. Urban 'regeneration': reflections on a metaphor. *Critical Social Policy*, 19(4), 419–45.

Garland, D. 2001. *The Culture of Control*. Oxford: Oxford University Press.

Giddens, A. 1994. *Beyond Left and Right*. Cambridge: Polity Press.

Giddens, A. 1998a. *The Third Way*. Cambridge: Polity Press.

Giddens, A. 1998b. The future of the welfare state, in *Is there a Third Way?* edited by M. Novak. London: IEA.

Giddens, A. 2000. *The Third Way and its Critics*. Cambridge: Polity Press.

Giddens, A. 2002. *Where Now for New Labour?* London: Fabian Society.

Ginsburg, N. 1999. Putting the social into urban regeneration policy. *Local Economy*, 14(1), 55–71.

Glen, A. 1993. Methods and Themes in Community Practice, in *Community and Public Policy*, edited by H. Butcher, A. Glen, P. Henderson and J. Smith, London: Pluto Press, 22–40.

Goes, E. 2004. The Third Way and the politics of community, in *The Third Way and Beyond: Criticisms, Futures and Alternatives*, edited by S. Hale, W. Leggett and L. Martell. Manchester: Manchester University Press, 108–27.

Gore, C. and Figueiredo, J. (eds). 1997. *Social Exclusion and Anti-poverty Policy: A Debate*. Geneva: International Labour Organisation.

Greener, I. 2002. Agency, social theory and social policy. *Critical Social Policy*, 22(4), 688–705.

Hall, S. 1998. The great moving nowhere show, *Marxism Today*. Nov/Dec., 9–14.

Hancock, L. 2001. *Community, Crime and Disorder*. Basingstoke: Palgrave.

Hastings, A. 2003. Strategic, multilevel neighbourhood regeneration: an outward looking approach at last? in *Urban Renaissance? New Labour, Community and Urban Policy*, edited by R. Imrie and M. Raco. Bristol: Policy Press, 85–100.

Hay, C. 1999. *The Political Economy of New Labour*. Manchester: Manchester University Press.

Herbert, S. 2005. The Trapdoor of Community. *Annals of the Association of American Geographers*, 95(4), 850–65.

Heron, E. 2001. Etzoni's spirit of communitarianism: community values and welfare realities in Blair's Britain, in *Social Policy Review 13*, edited by R. Sykes, C. Bochel and N. Ellison. Bristol: Policy Press, 63–82.

Heron, E. and Dwyer, P. 1999. Doing the Right Thing: Labour's attempt to forge a new welfare deal between the individual and the state. *Social Policy and Administration*, 33(1): 91–104.

Hibbitt, K., Jones, P. and Meegan, R. 2001. Tackling Social Exclusion: The role of social capital in urban regeneration on Merseyside – From mistrust to trust? *European Planning Studies*, 9(2), 141–61.

Hills, J., le Grand, J. and Piachaud, D. (eds). 2002. *Understanding Social Exclusion*. Oxford: Oxford University Press.

Hills, J. and Stewart, K. 2005. Introduction, in *A More Equal Society*, edited by J. Hills and K. Stewart. Bristol: Policy Press, 1–22.

HM Treasury. 2001a. *Tackling Child Poverty: A Pre-budget Report Document*. London: HMSO.

HM Treasury. 2001b. *The Changing Welfare State: Employment, Opportunity for All*. London: HMSO.

Hoban, M. 2001. Rethinking Regeneration. *Critical Social Policy*, 21(4), 519–22.

Hoban, M. and Beresford, P. 2001. Regenerating regeneration. *Community Development Journal*, 36(4), 312–20.

Hoggett, P. (ed). 1997. *Contested Communities: Experiences, Struggles, Policies*. Bristol: Policy Press.

Hoggett, P. 2000. *Emotional Life and the Politics of Welfare*. Basingstoke: Macmillan.

Hoggett. P. 2001. Agency, Rationality and Social Policy. *Journal of Social Policy*, 30(1), 37–56.

Home Office. 2002a. Sharpened tools will spearhead crackdown. Press Release, 12 November.

Home Office. 2002b. David Blunkett calls on communities to work together to combat youth crime. Press Release, 14 November.

Home Office. 2003. *Respect and Responsibility: Taking a Stand against Antisocial Behaviour*. London: Home Office.

Home Office. 2004. New powers to help communities continue crackdown on antisocial behaviour. Press release, 20 January.

Home Office. 2005. Rehabilitation for Neighbours from Hell. Press release 14 February.

Imrie, R. and Raco, M. (eds). 2003. *Urban Renaissance? New Labour, Community and Urban Policy*. Bristol: Policy Press.

Jessop, B. 2003. Governance and Metagovernance: on reflexivity, requisite variety, and requisite irony. Published by Department of Sociology, Lancaster University. Available at: http://www.lancs.ac.uk/fass/sociology/papers/jessop-governance-and-metagovernance.pdf [Accessed 2 March 2010].

John, P. 2009. Citizen governance: where it came from, what it is going, in *Changing Local Governance, Changing Citizens*, edited by C. Durose, S. Greasley and L. Richardson. Bristol: Policy Press.

Jordan, B. 1996. *A Theory of Poverty and Social Exclusion*. Bristol: Policy Press.

Jordan, B. 2005. New Labour: choice and values. *Critical Social Policy*, 25(4), 427–46.

JRF (Joseph Rowntree Foundation). 1999. 'Social cohesion and urban inclusion for disadvantaged neighbourhoods. Findings 4109, April. York: Joseph Rowntree Foundation.

JRF. 2002. Councillors warn that spread of partnership policies risks undermining local democracy. Press Release, 15 November.

Kearns, A. 2003. Social capital, regeneration and urban policy, in *Urban Renaissance? New Labour, Community and Urban Policy*, edited by R. Imrie and M. Raco. Bristol: Policy Press, 37–60.

Kearns, A. and Parkinson, M. 2001. The Significance of Neighbourhood. *Urban Studies*, 38(12), 2103–10.

Keegans Regeneration Ltd. 2003. *Neighbourhood Renewal Assessment of Charlestown and Lower Kersal NDC for Salford City Council.* Watford: Keegans Regeneration Ltd.

Kemshall, H. 2002. *Risk, Social Policy and Welfare*. Buckingham: Open University Press.

Kenrick, D. and Bakewell, S. 1990. *On the Verge: The Gypsies of England.* London: The Runnymede Trust.

Kooiman. J. 1999. Social–Political Governance, overview, reflections and design. *Public Management Review*, 1(1), 67–92.

Labour Party. 1997. General Election Manifesto. Labour Party.

Labour Party. 2001. General Election Manifesto. Labour Party.

Lawless, P. 1989. *Britain's Inner Cities.* 2nd edition. London: Paul Chapman Publishing.

Lawless, P. and Brown, F. 1986. *Urban Growth and Change in Britain: An Introduction.* London: Harper & Row.

Lawless, P., Foden, M., Wilson, I. and Beatty, C. 2009. Understanding Area-based Regeneration: The New Deal for Communities Programme in England. *Urban Studies*, 47(2), 257–75.

Le Grand, J. 2003. *Motivation, Agency and Public Policy.* Oxford: Oxford University Press.

Le Grand, J. and Richardson, L. 2002. Outsider and Insider Expertise: the response of residents of deprived neighbourhoods to an academic definition of social exclusion. CASE report. Available at: http://sticerd.lse.ac.uk/dps/case/cp/CASEpaper57.pdf.

Lee, M. 2001. *Childhood and Society.* Buckingham: Open University Press.

Levitas, R. 1998. *The Inclusive Society? Social Exclusion and New Labour.* Basingstoke: Palgrave.

Levitas, R. 2000. Community, utopia and New Labour. *Local Economy*, 15(3), 188–97.

Levitas, R. 2001. Government more concerned with conformity than poverty. *The Guardian*, 23 March.

Lister, R. 1998. From Equality to Social Inclusion: New Labour and the Welfare State. *Critical Social Policy*, 18(2), 215–25.

Lister, R. 1999. First Steps to a Fairer Society. *The Guardian*, 9 June.

Lister, R. 2000. To RIO via the third way: Labour's 'welfare reform agenda'. *Renewal*, 8(4), 9–20.

Lister, R. 2001. New Labour: a study in ambiguity from a position of ambivalence. *Critical Social Policy*, 21(4), 425–47.

Lister, R. 2002. A Politics of Recognition and Respect: involving people with experience of poverty in decision making that affects their lives. *Social Policy and Society*, 1(1), 37–46.

Lister, R. 2004. *Poverty*. Cambridge: Polity Press.

Lister, R. 2006. Children (but not women) first: New Labour, child welfare and gender. *Critical Social Policy*, 26(2), 315–35.

Lovering, J. 1995. Creating discourses rather than jobs: the crisis in the cities and the transition fantasies of intellectuals and policymakers, in *Managing Cities: The New Urban Context*, edited by P. Healey, S. Cameron, S. Davondi, S. Graham and A. Madanipour. Chichester: John Wiley & Sons, 109–26.

Lowndes, V. and Sullivan, H. 2008. How low can you go? Rationales and challenges for neighbourhood governance. *Public Administration*, 86(1), 53–74.

Lund, B. 1999a. Ask not what your community can do for you: obligations, New Labour and welfare reform. *Critical Social Policy*, 19(4), 447–62.

Lund, B. 1999b. The Poor in a Loomp is Bad: New Labour and Neighbourhood Renewal. *Political Quarterly*, 70(3), 280–84.

Lupton, R. 2003. *Poverty Street: The Dynamics of Neighbourhood Decline and Renewal*. Bristol: Policy Press.

Lupton, R. and Power, A. 2002. Social Exclusion and Neighbourhoods, in *Understanding Social Exclusion*, edited by J. Hills, J. le Grand and D. Pichaud. Oxford: Oxford University Press, 118–40.

Lupton, R. and Power, A. 2005. Disadvantaged by where you live? New Labour and neighbourhood renewal, in *A More Equal Society?* edited by J. Hills and K. Stewart. Bristol: Policy Press, 119–42.

MacLeavy, J. 2009. (Re)analyzing community empowerment: rationalities and technologies of government in Bristol's New Deal for Communities. *Urban Studies*, 46(4), 849–45.

Makyut, P. and Morehouse, R. 1994. *Beginning Social Research: A Philosophical and Practical Guide*. London: Routledge Falmer.

Manchester Evening News. 2003. Reference unknown.

Mandelson, P. 1997. *Labour's Next Steps: Tackling Social Exclusion*. London: Fabian Society.

Mann, K. 1992. *The Making of an English 'Underclass'?* Buckingham: Open University Press.

Mann, K. 1998. Lamppost modernism: traditional and critical social policy. *Critical Social Policy*, 18(1), 77–102.

Mann, K. 2003. The schlock and the new: risk, reflexivity and retirement, in *Social Policy Review* 15, edited by C. Bochel, N. Ellison and M. Powell. Bristol: Policy Press, 217–38.

Marinetto, M. 2003. Who wants to be an active citizen? The politics and practice of community involvement. *Sociology*, 37, 103–20.

Marquand, D. 1996. Moralists and Hedonists, in *The Ideas that Shaped Post-War Britain*, edited by D. Marquand and A. Seldon. London: Fontana.

Massey, D. 2004. Geographies of Responsibility. *Geografiska Annaler, Series B*: Human Geography, 86(1), 5–18.

McCullen, P. and Harris, C. 2004. Generative equality and the Third Way: a managerial perspective, in *The Third Way and Beyond: Criticisms, Futures and Alternatives*, edited by S. Hale, W. Leggett and L. Martell. Manchester: Manchester University Press, 48–63.

Miliband, D. 2006. *Change the World*. Speech to The Fabian Society. 19 January. Available at http://www.davidmiliband.info/speeches/speeches_08_01.htm [Accessed 27 February 2010].

Mooney, G. and Fyfe, N. 2006. New Labour and the community protests: the case of the Govanhill swimming pool campaign. *Local Economy*, 21(2), 136–50.

Morris, L. 1994. *Dangerous Classes: The Underclass and Social Citizenship*. London: Routledge.

Morrison, Z. 2003. Cultural justice addressing social exclusion: a case study of a Single Regeneration Budget project in Blackbird Leys, Oxford, in *Urban Renaissance? New Labour, Community and Urban Policy*, edited by R. Imrie and M. Raco. Bristol: Policy Press, 139–62.

Moulaert, F. 1995. Measuring socioeconomic disintegration at the local level in Europe: an analytical framework, in *Beyond the Threshold: The Measurement and Analysis of Social Exclusion*, edited by G. Room. Bristol: Policy Press, 1–9.

Naughtie, J. 2002. *The Rivals*. London: Fourth Estate.

Newman, J. (ed.) 2001. *Modernizing Governance: New Labour, Policy and Society*. London: Sage.

Newman, J. and Clarke, J. 2009. *Publics, Politics and Power: Remaking the Public in Public Services*. London: Sage.

NRU (Neighbourhood Renewal Unit). 2001. *Annual Review of New Deal for Communities*. London: TSO.

NRU. 2002. *NDC Elections: a study in community engagement*. London: TSO.

NRU. 2005. *Research report 17: NDC 2001–2005 an interim evaluation*. London: TSO.

Office of the Deputy Prime Minister (ODPM). 2000. *Our Towns and Cities: The Future, Delivering an Urban Renaissance*. London: TSO.

ODPM. 2005. *Key findings summary: new localism – citizen engagement, neighbourhoods and public services: evidence from local government*. London: TSO.

Onxy, J. and Benton, P. 1995. Empowerment and Ageing: Toward Honoured Places for Crones and Sages, in *Community Empowerment: A Reader in Participation and Development*, edited by G. Craig and M. Mayo. London: Zed Books, 46–58.

Osbourne, T. and Rose, N. 2004. Spatial Phenomenotecnics: making space with Charles Booth and Patrick Geddes. *Environment and Planning D*, 22(2), 209–28.

Orwell, G. 2001. *The Road to Wigan Pier*. London: Penguin Classics.

Oxfam. 2005. No more sticky dots: making progress with participatory appraisal in Salford. Available at http://publications.oxfam.org.uk/oxfam/display.asp?K=002X0016 [Accessed 10 June 2009].

Page, D. 2002. *Communities in the Balance: The Reality of Social Exclusion on Housing Estates*. York: Joseph Rowntree Foundation.

Page, R. 2007. Without a Song in their Heart: New Labour, the Welfare State and the Retreat from Democratic Socialism. *Journal of Social Policy*, 36(1), 19–37.

Parry, J. 2005. Care in the Community? Gender and the reconfiguration of community work in a post-mining neighbourhood. *Sociological Review*, 53(4), 149–66.

Payne, G. 1992. Community and community studies. *Sociology Review*, 4(1), 16–19.

Percy-Smith, J. (ed.). 2000. *Policy Responses to Social Exclusion: Towards Inclusion?* Buckingham: Open University Press.

Pereira, C. 1997. Anthology: The Breadth of Community, in *Community Care: A Reader*, edited by J. Bornat et al. London: Macmillan.

Phillips, T. and Smith, P. 2003. Everyday Incivility: towards a benchmark. *The Sociological Review*, 15(1), 85–108.

Powell, M. (ed.). 1999. *New Labour, New Welfare State?* Bristol: Policy Press.

Powell, M. 2000. Something old, something new, something borrowed, something blue: the jackdaw politics of the Third Way. *Renewal*, 8(4), 21–31.

Powell, M. (ed.). 2002. *Evaluating New Labour's Welfare Reforms*. Bristol: Policy Press.

Power, A. and Wilmott, H. 2005. Bringing up families in poor neighbourhoods under New Labour, in *A More Equal Society*, edited by J. Hills and K. Stewart. Bristol: Policy Press, 277–96.

Prideaux, S. 2001. New Labour, Old Functionalism: The underlying contradictions of welfare reform in the US and the UK. *Social Policy and Administration*, 35(1), 85–115.

Prideaux, S. 2004. From Organisational Theory to the Third Way: The Continuities and Contradictions Underpinning Amitai Etzioni's Communitarian Influence on New Labour, in *The Third Way and Beyond: Criticisms, Futures and*

Alternatives, edited by S. Hale, W. Leggett and L. Martell. Manchester: Manchester University Press, 128–46.

Prideaux, S. 2005. *Not so New Labour.* Bristol: Policy Press.

Prior, D. 2005. Civil renewal and community safety: Virtuous policy spiral or dynamic of exclusion. *Social Policy and Society*, 4(4), 357–67.

Puttnam, R. 2000. *Bowling Alone: The Collapse and Revival of American Community.* New York: Simon & Schuster.

Ramrayka, L. 2000. Through brick walls. *The Guardian*, 5 July.

Respect Task Force. 2006. *Respect Action Plan.* London: TSO.

Rhodes, R.A.W. 1996. The new governance: governing without government. *Political Studies*, 44, 652–67.

Richardson, L. and Mumford, K. 2002. Community, Neighbourhood and Social Infrastructure, in *Understanding Social Exclusion*, edited by J. Hills, J. le Grand and D. Pichaud. Oxford: Oxford University Press, 202–25.

Roberts, R. 1971. *The Classic Slum.* Manchester: Manchester University Press.

Robinson, F. and Shaw, K. 1992. Urban regeneration and community development. *Local Economy*, 6(4), 71–2.

Room, G. (ed.) 1995. *Beyond the Threshold. The Measurement and Analysis of Social Exclusion.* Bristol: Policy Press.

Room, G. 1995. Conclusions, in *Beyond the Threshold. The Measurement and Analysis of Social Exclusion*, edited by G. Room. Bristol: Policy Press, 233–47.

Rose, N. 1996a. Identity, Genealogy, History, in *Questions of Cultural Identity*, edited by S. Hall and P. du Gay. London: Sage, 128–50.

Rose, N. 1996b. The death of the social? Refiguring the territory of government. *Economy and Society*, 25(3), 327–56.

Rose, N. 1999. *Governing the Soul.* 2nd edition. London: Free Association.

Rose, N. 2000. Community, citizenship and the Third Way. *American Behavioural Scientist*, 43(9), 1395–1411.

Rouse, J. and Smith, G. 2002. Evaluating New Labour's accountability reforms, in *Evaluating New Labour's Welfare Reforms*, edited by M. Powell. Bristol: Policy Press, 39–60.

Rowe, M. and Devanney, C. 2003. Partnership and the governance of regeneration. *Critical Social Policy*, 23(3), 375–97.

Salford City Council. Available at: http://www.salford.gov.uk/council/elections. htm.

Salford Partnership. 2002. *Regenerating a Great City: Salford's Neighbourhood Renewal Strategy.* Salford: Salford City Council.

Scammel, M. 2003. Citizen Consumers: Towards a New Marketing of Politics, in *Media and the Restyling of Politics*, edited by J. Corner and D. Pels. London: Sage, 117–36.

Social Exclusion Unit (SEU). 1998. *Bringing Britain Together: A National Strategy for Neighbourhood Renewal.* London: TSO.

SEU. 2000. *Report of Policy Action Team 8: Antisocial Behaviour.* London: TSO.

SEU. 2001a. *A New Commitment to Neighbourhood Renewal: National Strategy Action Plan*. London: TSO.

SEU. 2001b. *Preventing Social Exclusion*. London: TSO.

Somerville, P. 2005. Community governance and democracy. *Policy and Politics*, 33(1), 117–44.

Squires, P. 1990. *Anti-Social Policy: Welfare, Ideology and the Disciplinary State*. Hemel Hempstead: Harvester Wheatsheaf.

Squires, P. 2006. New Labour and the politics of antisocial behaviour. *Critical Social Policy*, 26(1), 144–68.

Squires, P. and Stephen, D. 2005. Rethinking ASBOs. *Critical Social Policy*, 25(4), 517–28.

Stedman Jones, G. 1971. *Outcast London*. Oxford: Oxford University Press.

Stoker, G. (ed.). 2000. *The New Politics of British Local Governance*. London: Macmillan.

Swyngedouw, E. 2005. Governance innovation and the citizen: the janus face of governance-beyond-the-state. *Urban Studies*, 42(11), 1991–2006.

Taylor, G. (ed.). 1999. *The Impact of New Labour*. Basingstoke: Macmillan Press.

Taylor, M. 1995. Community Work and the State: The Changing Context of UK Practice, in *Community Empowerment: A Reader in Participation and Development*, edited by G. Craig and M. Mayo. London: Zed Books, 99–111.

Taylor, M. 2000a. Communities in the lead: power, organisational capacity and social capital. *Urban Studies*, 37(5–6), 1019–35.

Taylor, M. 2000b. Maintaining community involvement in regeneration: what are the issues? *Local Economy*, 15(3), 251–67.

Taylor, M. 2003. *Public Policy in the Community*. London: Palgrave.

Taylor, M. 2007. Community participation in the real world: opportunities and pitfalls in new governance spaces. *Urban Studies*, 44(2), 297–317.

Taylor, P. 1999. Places, spaces and Macy's: place-spaces tensions in the political geography of modernities. *Progress in Human Geography*, 23(1), 7–26.

Tönnies, F. 1967. *Community and Society*. Michigan: Michigan University Press.

Toynbee, P. 2003 Promises for the poor. *The Guardian*, 11 April.

Toynbee, P. and Walker, D. 2005. *Better or Worse? Has Labour Delivered?* London: Bloomsbury.

Wallace, A. 2007. 'We've had nothing for so long that we don't know what to ask for' New Labour and the regeneration of socially excluded terrain. *Social Policy and Society*, 6(1), 1–12.

Wallace, A. 2009. Governance at a distance? The turn to the local in UK social policy, in *Social Policy Review 21*, edited by E. Rummery, I. Greener and C. Holden. Bristol: Policy Press, 245–66.

Wallace, A. 2010 (early view) New Neighbourhoods, New Citizens? Challenging 'Community' as a Framework for Social and Moral Regeneration under New Labour in the UK, *International Journal of Urban and Regional Research*, 34(3).

Warwick, D. and Littlejohn, G. *Coal, Capital and Culture.* London: Routledge.

Weaver, M. 2002. Friction slows the New Deal. *The Guardian*, 20 February.

White, R. 2003. Communities, conferences and restorative social justice. *Criminal Justice*, 3(2), 139–60.

White, S. 1999. Rights and Responsibilities: a social democratic perspective, in *The New Social Democracy*, edited by A. Gamble and T. Wright. Oxford: Blackwell, 166–79.

White, S. (ed.). 2001. *New Labour The Progressive Future?* Basingstoke: Palgrave.

White, S. 2003. *The Civic Minimum.* Oxford: Oxford University Press.

Whitehead. 2003. 'In the shadow of hierarchy': meta-governance, policy reform and urban regeneration in the West Midlands. *Area*, 35(1), 6–14.

Wilks-Heeg, S. 2003. Economy, equity or empowerment? New Labour, communities and urban policy evaluation, in *Urban Renaissance? New Labour, Community and Urban Policy* edited by R. Imrie and M. Raco. Bristol: Policy Press, 205–19.

Williams, F. 1997. Women and Community, in *Community Care: A Reader*, edited by J. Bornat. London: Macmillan.

Williams, F. 1999. Exploring Links Between Old and New Paradigms – A Critical Review, in *Welfare Research: A Critical Review*, edited by F. Williams, J. Popay and A. Oakley. London: UCL Press, 18–42.

Williams, F. 2001. In and Beyond New Labour: Towards a New Political Ethics of Care. *Critical Social Policy*, 21(4), 467–93.

Williams, F., Popay, J. and Oakley, A. 1999. Changing Paradigms of Welfare, in *Welfare Research: A Critical Review*, edited by F. Williams, J. Popay and A. Oakley. London: UCL Press, 2–15.

Williams, F. and Popay, J. 1999. Balancing Polarities: Developing a New Framework for Welfare Research, in *Welfare Research: A Critical Review*, edited by F. Williams, J. Popay and A. Oakley. London: UCL Press, 156–82.

Williamson, J. 2002. Tough on horridness. *The Guardian*, 14 November.

Wilson, J.Q. 1993. *The Moral Sense.* New York: Macmillan.

Wilson, W.J. 1987. *The Truly Disadvantaged: The Inner City, the Underclass and Public Policy.* Chicago: Chicago University Press.

Wintour, P. 2003. Blunkett goes back to his roots to fight disorder. *The Guardian*, 12 March.

Worley, C. 2005. 'It's not about race. It's about the community': New Labour and 'community cohesion'. *Critical Social Policy*, 25(4), 483–96.

Young, M. and Willmott, P. 1957. *Family and Kinship in East London.* London: Routledge and Kegan Paul.

Index

For Product Safety Concerns and Information please contact our EU
representative GPSR@taylorandfrancis.com
Taylor & Francis Verlag GmbH, Kaufingerstraße 24, 80331 München, Germany

9 781138 251540